P9-CDA-644

# Green Zone Selling

**How Top Producing Salespeople Out-sell,
Out-earn and Outlast Everyone Else**

Douglas Smith

authorHOUSE®

*AuthorHouse*™
*1663 Liberty Drive*
*Bloomington, IN 47403*
*www.authorhouse.com*
*Phone: 1-800-839-8640*

© *2011 Douglas Smith. All rights reserved.*

*No part of this book may be reproduced, stored in a retrieval system, or transmitted by any means without the written permission of the author.*

*First published by AuthorHouse 7/28/2011*

*ISBN: 978-1-4634-2250-9 (e)*
*ISBN: 978-1-4634-2251-6 (hc)*
*ISBN: 978-1-4634-2252-3 (sc)*

*Library of Congress Control Number: 2011909581*

*Printed in the United States of America*

*Any people depicted in stock imagery provided by Thinkstock are models, and such images are being used for illustrative purposes only. Certain stock imagery © Thinkstock.*

*This book is printed on acid-free paper.*

*Because of the dynamic nature of the Internet, any web addresses or links contained in this book may have changed since publication and may no longer be valid. The views expressed in this work are solely those of the author and do not necessarily reflect the views of the publisher, and the publisher hereby disclaims any responsibility for them.*

*For Andy and Laurel*

# Let's Get Started!

If the three most important words in a relationship are "I love you" then the three most important words in selling are "Let's get started." Say that out loud right now:

*Let's get started!*

Doesn't that sound great? You walk into a meeting and say: "Good morning everyone. Let's get started!" You're delivering a presentation to a group of prospects and you open with: "Thank you for coming. Let's get started." A customer says he is interested in your offer. Your response? "Fantastic. Let's get started!" Wow! These three words say a lot about who you are. They say you are ready to do business, ready to take action, ready to help. Does that sound like a winning sales professional? You bet.

Great salespeople get things started. They waste little time. They are anxious people always thinking forward and moving ahead. They know that talk is cheap, time is money and action is everything. So let me practice what I preach when it comes to this book and our goal to make you an even better salesperson tomorrow than you are today:

***Let's get started!***

# Welcome to the Green Zone

Have you ever been on a "sales high?" You know the feeling; positive things are happening, goals are being accomplished, your customers are happy and you are making great money.

That's the "Green Zone" of selling. That's where top producers live and that's where you'll find job security, happiness and all the money and recognition you could ever want. The Green Zone is where you want to be.

Every salesperson I've ever met—even the most successful ones—wants to be more successful and make more money. (Let's test this observation right now: Raise your hand if you'd like to be *less* successful and earn *less* money. I didn't think so.) Even if you are doing well right now, even though you may be a highly-experienced salesperson, even if you are proud of your track record and present standing, you likely want to be even more successful and make even more money going forward. Am I right? To improve your success and make more money, there are some things you have to do that you are not currently doing. Here's a consistent message you will hear loud and clear throughout this book:

*Becoming an even greater success in selling requires "movement."*

Success isn't going to come find you; you have to *move* to find it. It's this action-oriented way of thinking and working that drives the most successful and highest paid salespeople in the world. Question: Are you ready to start moving?

In my live sales seminars, I sometimes flash up a big, bright green screen asking: "Quick! What does this color make you think of?" I always get the same two answers: "go" and "money." For most everybody, a green light is a signal meaning go and the word green is synonymous with money. That's exactly the point I want to make to my audiences—and to you in this book—how "go" and "money" are linked together. Again; it's about *movement*. The sales opportunities are out there and the money is too, I promise you. You just have to move to get it!

Together we'll be exploring the four key "zones" of *Green Zone Selling*:

- **The Mind Zone.** Top producers live in a different state of mind than do average or below-average producers. They think differently, hold different attitudes and outlooks and see their jobs and careers in ways others don't. The first step to achieving greater success in your sales career is to move your mind deep into the Green Zone. It is from there everything else springs into action.

- **The Time Zone.** How you spend your time and who you spend it with have a major impact on your chances for success. If you are a commissioned salesperson, you are essentially trading your time for money every day. When you invest the right amount of time with the right people doing the right things, you are working productively and profitably in the Green Zone.

- **The Contact Zone.** This is where the rubber meets the road. Sales happen when you finally get face-to-face or voice-to-voice with a customer. When you are in this critical moment, do you know what to say and how to say it? Great personal selling skills are a crucial characteristic of top producers. Those skilled in the art and science of interacting with their customers— connecting with people, listening to their needs, asking questions, providing clear, on-target solutions and advancing opportunities by asking for action—are always the highest paid and most successful salespeople. They are selling in the Green Zone.

- **The Future Zone.** You are where you are right now in your career because of what you have done—or not done—to this point. To get where you want to be tomorrow, next year, or five years from now, you have to do something different. I'll show you precisely how to take the steps that will lead you to that proverbial "next level" we all like to talk about. When you are focused on the future and taking specific actions to achieve your long-term career vision, you are moving forward in the Green Zone.

# On Your Mark! Get Set! Go!

By the way, I admire you. We may have never met, but I know something about you already. The fact that you spent money to buy this book and that you are taking the time to read what I have to say tells me that you are serious about success.

Since I value your time, I'll not waste a word. I'm going to jump right in. I have spent 30 years around sales professionals and found they are eager, restless people who grow impatient with wordy dialogue, overly-complex strategies, silly parables and sappy, motivational schlock. That's why you'll find none of that in the pages, lessons and ideas that follow.

**On your mark!** I know something else about you. *You are not where you want to be.* If you were already on top of your sales game, making oodles of money and getting everything you want, you wouldn't be reading my book. Correct? Let me make some assumptions about you right from the get-go:

- You want to close more sales and earn more money
- You want to be more secure in your job and career
- You want to be better organized so you can get more done in less time
- You want to feel valued and respected by your peers, your company and your boss
- You want to go to work every day truly enjoying what you do for a living

Did I get any of that right? It's my guess that you want *more* of something out of your career in sales. Good; I'm banking on that. Not willing to settle for what you have and wanting more are the first steps to becoming more successful at selling (or anything else for that matter.)

So here's the deal: For me to help get you where you want to be, you have to be honest about where you are now. I'm serious. You can't fix a problem you can't see—or won't allow yourself to see. You and I will be able to move forward when you are ready to admit that: 1) You have the potential to be more successful than you are today and 2) Some of the reasons why you are not more successful are because of you.

I'll ask you to take some self-assessments. I'll present some rather pointed questions and require you to perform a few brief exercises. If you can be completely honest with yourself I can take you forward in your career, help you get better at selling and earn more money in the process. Can you do that? Can you be honest with yourself? Good, then I can take you deep into the Green Zone—that place of positive forward movement (go) and far more riches (money).

**Get set!** Prepare yourself mentally for an exciting, engaging journey. I will do everything possible to take you from where you are now in your sales career to where you want to be. Just remember this:

*You can't get someplace different until you leave where you are.*

If you like your current standing in your sales career then do nothing different. Put this book in the recycle bin (better yet, give it to a colleague) and go back to what you were doing. To *get* something different you have to be willing to *do* something different. That requires you to perform an act many people are afraid to do; *change.* You must be willing to leave familiar ground, say goodbye to bad habits, even exit relationships with certain clients and co-workers that could be holding you back. You must realize that what got you where you are today may not get you to where you want to be tomorrow. Can you agree with that? Are you capable of changing?

**Go!** They say that knowledge is power. But knowledge by itself won't transform you. Only action transforms. To become a success or stay a success in selling you need that all-important, action-oriented "movement" mindset. You must be able to put into play the ideas and approaches I will share with you. This book will not make you a success in selling; what you apply from this book will. If you implement what you learn and practice these lessons routinely you will achieve success in your selling career you can't even imagine. That's a promise I'll make to you right from the start.

You are where you are because of what you have done—or not done—to this point. If you want *more* money, *more* success, *more* recognition, *more* freedom and *more* job security, then it is clear you must do something *more*, something different. It's called change. And the first thing you may need to change is your mind. How you think about yourself, your abilities, your profession and your future dictate the direction you take every day.

Are you ready? Here we go.

# Table of Contents

# Part One

## The Mind Zone

# Think and Grow Rich

In 1937, Napoleon Hill published his landmark work *Think and Grow Rich*. It became one of the most influential books of all time pointing the way to personal achievement and financial freedom. Today, 75 years later, it remains a best seller among business and self-help books.

*Think and Grow Rich* was inspired by American magnate Andrew Carnegie, who disclosed his own fundamentals and formulas for success to the author. Carnegie's ideas, reflected through Hill's book, inspired scores of others to adopt a series of simple "how to" approaches and become successful businesspeople and millionaires themselves. (When you are finished with this book you should buy that one and read it cover-to-cover. It's potent stuff.)

The premise for *Think and Grow Rich* sets the stage for the lessons taught in *Green Zone Selling*. It can be summarized in just one sentence:

*If you can change your mind, you can change your life.*

Your mind is the navigator of your life, and in our case here, your career in selling. Your mind will tell you what to think, where to go, and how to behave. Your mind is responsible for where you are today because of what it has told you to *believe*. If you are trying to move to someplace different (more success, more customers, more income, more happiness) then you must begin to condition your mind to believe in something different.

There are some salespeople who don't believe they can achieve more. They don't believe they can move past the present and enjoy a better future. They don't believe it is possible to become a top performer in their company, or that they can make a six-figure income in selling. That is precisely why they never will. It is their lack of *belief* that stymies their results—or torpedoes their careers altogether.

Andrew Carnegie believed emphatically that he would be an enormous success and that his business ideas were valid. He believed in America, he believed in the vast opportunities out there, and he believed in himself. When you read *Think and Grow Rich* you will be continually reminded of the power of the mind and how your thoughts and belief system will dictate what you do today and what you will become tomorrow.

So what do you believe? What is your mind telling you right now? Here are a few questions I'd like you to answer:

1. Do you believe in your abilities as a salesperson?
2. Do you believe you are performing at your peak potential?
3. Do you believe there are more sales opportunities out there right now?
4. Do you believe you have learned all there is to learn about professional selling?
5. Do you believe you can change?

The last question is what I call the "killer" question. *Do you truly believe you can change?* Can you move to a new mindset? For you to get in and stay in the Green Zone of success from here on, it is essential that you can. It's no secret that change isn't easy for a lot of people. Want proof?

# The Pain of Change

I once read an amazing article in a science magazine that someone left on an airplane. This is the gist of that story.

There was a small tribe of primitive people living in a remote jungle in South America. Explorers had discovered their village years ago and apart from visits by a few doctors and missionaries the decision was made to respect the tribe's culture and keep the natives isolated by having as little contact with them as possible.

Then, one of the members of the tribe mysteriously died. Soon another fell ill and died, and then another. The doctors and missionaries stepped in to uncover what was happening. They found that some form of toxin had contaminated the soil and that the village could no longer sustain itself on the land where they and their ancestors had lived for hundreds of years.

An alternative site was found and the mission workers tried to persuade the tribe to move to a new location about twenty miles away from the poisoned ground. The people refused. They understood what was happening and that the land would kill them if they remained, but they were so fearful of change they would not budge. The story has an unhappy ending; the entire village died. Wiped out. Their lineage no longer exists. These people were so frightened of the unknown that they chose to perish rather than face change.

Do you get the point?

# Why You Must Change

The sad situation of the jungle tribe mirrors that of a lot of people in selling today. Many salespeople are so afraid of change or are so unwilling to transform themselves that they virtually choose to "die" in their jobs and careers altogether. In effect, they would rather fail than change.

Remember what I said earlier: You are where you are today— your income, sales performance, job security, everything—as a result of what you have done so far. You have created your current world. If you are happy and successful and making great money, good for you. You've earned it. If you are not happy or successful and not making great money, it is your fault. You can point the finger of blame in many directions: your company isn't supporting you, your price is too high, there's too much competition out there, the technology you have is antiquated, the economy stinks, blah, blah, blah. I'm not buying it because you can't sell it. Want proof? How come others in your company, in your industry, in this economy, with many of the same challenges you cite as excuses are out-performing and out-earning you right now? Well? How come?

Perhaps that little jab upset you. Well, I'm sorry. From time to time I will irritate you, challenge your way of thinking, even call your bluff. That's my job as your "coach" throughout this book. You see, I'm trying to break down what could be *years* of incorrect thinking and preconceived notions you have about selling, about yourself, and about your chances for success. I am attempting to alter your belief system from here on. To do that, I'm going to play on your emotions sometimes. It's for the best—your best.

So the biggest thing I'm going to confront you on is this: *if you are not where you want to be, you have to change.* Albert Einstein defined insanity as conducting the same experiment the same way again and again and expecting a different outcome. A lot of "insane" salespeople keep doing the same thing day after day and expect a different result. If you want something different (more success, more sales, more money) you have to do something different; there is no alternative.

You may discover that some of what I present in this book are attitudes and actions foreign to you. You may need to change some of your sales strategies, how you approach customers, even how you think about selling as a whole. Do this, make these changes, and you will find yourself producing bigger results, earning more money and enjoying more job security and happiness. Hey—aren't those things worth changing for?

Most struggling or average-performing salespeople struggle

or stay average because of their unwillingness to change or improve themselves. They say they want more, but they are not willing to do anything more or different to get what they want. They say: "I'm going to just keep plugging along," or "I'll just continue to do what I have been doing." That's why they never get ahead. That's why they never make more money. That's why they never taste real success. *They don't change!*

I deliver around 100 sales seminars each year. Each time as I look out over my audience of participants, I am haunted by the fact that perhaps eight out of ten of them will never apply a single thing I teach them. Most of them want more, but most of them won't do what they need to do to get it. Again, they won't change.

Vow right now that you will not be one of these people! Open your mind to change and accept it as a part of your career growth, let alone your survival in the business world. As Charles Darwin so notably observed in his landmark work *The Origin of Species:*

> *"It is not the strongest of species that survives, or the most intelligent. It is the ones that can best adapt to change."*

# Green Zone Selling

As we move through this book, we'll stop every few pages and review the most important lessons you are learning. So far these would be:

**» Your belief system controls how you think and what you do. If you can change your mind for the better, you change your life for the best. The first step to becoming an even greater success in selling is the belief that you can.**

**» A fear of change or an unwillingness to change can—and often will—kill your career and your chances for success.**

**» You are where you are because of what you have done or not done to this point. Be open and honest in assessing your strengths and weaknesses and where you need to change.**

Use these summary boxes as a quick review guide later on. For now, let's keep moving...

# Joining the Top Twenty Percent

Vilfredo Pareto was an Italian economist living in the early 1900s. At the time, European countries like Italy, France and England saw themselves as very wealthy—among the richest countries in the world. Pareto didn't see it. As he traveled across Europe he observed a lot of poverty and individuals living in meager, even spartan conditions. So, Pareto set out on a little research project. What he found was astonishing.

Pareto discovered that when you add up all the wealth in most any European country, indeed there was a lot of it. However, his studies showed that roughly 80 percent of a country's wealth was controlled by just 20 percent of the population, and that the other 80 percent of the people own only 20 percent of the wealth. This became widely known throughout Europe as The Pareto Principle. Today we refer to this phenomenon as The 80/20 Rule.

While not an exact science, The 80/20 Rule is remarkably applicable in selling. In my experience managing, training and working with sales teams and organizations over many years, I have found that in nearly every case 80 percent of the total sales in any company or team are generated by the top 20 percent of the salespeople who work there. The wealth, results and success are not equally distributed. The top 20 percent are highly successful and making very good money (thriving in the Green Zone) while the other 80 percent do okay or barely get by month after month. There are few "middle class" salespeople. They are either crushing it (the top 20 percent) or they are chugging along and fighting for every deal they can get (the other 80 percent). I have seen this disparity hundreds of times in large organizations and small firms. It is likely true in the company or sales team where you work. Am I right?

Remember I said earlier that knowledge may be power, but only action transforms. Knowing Pareto's 80/20 Rule is interesting and powerful, but what do you do with it? Here's what you do:

*You must become one of the top 20 percent of the*
*salespeople in your company or your industry.*

The top 20 percent of all salespeople control the bulk of the business, the wealth and the success. Eight out of ten deals, contracts or sales are written by the same top 20 percent of the salespeople month after month. Everyone else is just making a marginal income, struggling, or failing altogether. If you want to do well in sales, you must be in the top 20 percent... period.

If you are a car salesman at an auto dealership and there are 50 salespeople, you must be in the top ten. If you are a real estate agent in a market of 2,500 other agents, you must be in the top 500. If you work in telecom sales and there are 30 sales reps in your group, you must be among the top six. If you are in the top 20 percent now, work hard to stay there. If you are not on the top 20 percent now, work hard to move there. It is within this elite group you will find more money, more happiness, more job security, more recognition, and more long-term success.

For you to get in that coveted top 20 percent, you have to know the threshold for entry. This is where a bit of investigative research pays off. Do some digging. Talk to your boss. Get the facts. Find out (don't guess) the exact sales figure it takes each month to land you in the top 20 percent of your company, market or industry. Is it five sales? Is it 25 sales? You can't shoot for the top 20 percent if you don't know what it is. Go find out today.

The Pareto Principle is a powerful guide to success in sales. Get your mind in the right place for where you need to be. Start shooting for the top 20 percent. But before you do that, let me teach you another lesson—a lesson you might not want to learn and one that might be a bit painful for you to accept. (So there, you are forewarned!)

# Success Isn't Easy

I might as well get to this now, before it's too late. I'm going to make perhaps the most important point of the entire book right here, so pay close attention.

*Success in selling isn't easy to achieve.*

A lot of people want to believe that success is easy and that if they just apply themselves a bit more, work a little harder or make one more sales call a day, they will reach a higher level of income and results. Wrong; it's not that easy. It's just not. It would be great if it was, but it's not.

In the past you may have been exposed to books and seminars that proclaim: "Five Easy Steps to Success in Selling" or "How to Become an Overnight Success in Sales!" Maybe even your own sales manager has told you: "You'd be a top producer if you would just put in more hours." Your boss is wrong; it's just not that easy.

Success is *hard*. There, I said it. Success…is…hard. This is why the majority (80 percent) of all salespeople never achieve success—because it's hard. If success were easy, every salesperson would be successful and we wouldn't have the 80/20 Rule in play, right? It's not easy. It's hard. Why do you think so many salespeople struggle? Because success is hard. Why are so many mediocre salespeople making mediocre money? Because success is hard. Why do most sales teams experience a 40 to 70 percent turnover every year? Because success is hard.

Notice I'm not saying that *selling* is hard. Selling isn't hard; nearly anyone can sell and millions do. (It's the oldest profession!) I said that *success* in selling is hard. Everyone who gets into selling expects to do well; nobody plans to fail or just be middle-of-the-road. What most soon figure out is that while just about anyone can sell, not everyone can be *successful*

11

at selling. Why? Because success in selling is hard. (Have I pounded this nail enough already?)

There are dozens of components to being a success in selling. Among these are:

- Your mindset
- Your belief system
- Your commitment
- Luck
- Timing
- Your personality
- Your company's reputation
- Your products and services
- Your boss
- Your support team
- The economic climate
- The competition
- Your IQ
- Your selling skills
- Your discipline
- Your drive

I'm going to stop there because this list could go on for another two pages and by now you're just flying through the bullets.

Success in selling isn't easy to achieve and it is not just one thing that makes successful salespeople successful. Success is more like a formula or a recipe. You have to possess a lot of ingredients to become and remain a success in selling...or anything else for that matter.

What made Jack Nicklaus such a great golfer? Why is Abe Lincoln the leader so many admire? What turned Madonna into a worldwide sensation? In every case, it's certainly more than just one thing.

Are you okay with what I am teaching you now? I hope so.

You may have picked up this book thinking you were about to learn the "easy way" to success or maybe you would find that "one thing" to help you land more customers and earn more money without exerting much effort. Well, I must be honest with you; it's not here.

In the 30 years I've been involved in the world of sales, I've come to accept there are no secrets or shortcuts to success in selling and there is no one simple solution to most salespeople's performance problems. Success in selling is complex, it's challenging and it is hard. Believe it or not, that's good. Why is that good? It's good because it filters out thousands of people from the profession immediately. Success—being difficult to achieve and requiring numerous traits, skills and characteristics—eliminates 80 percent (maybe more) of your competition who are not willing to do, learn and apply all that it takes to be a success.

To continue this journey with me, you must get completely comfortable with this concept. Stop looking for the take-a-pill shortcut to success and start looking for the whole formula. I'll help you find it. I'll take you through the most important ingredients to a successful selling career. We've already found a few. We'll find more as we go deeper into The Mind Zone.

# Do You Really Belong in Sales?

Want to see something cool? The next time you fly through the Atlanta, Georgia airport and you have an extra fifteen minutes, take the tram to International Concourse E. Go up the escalator and walk down to Gate E3. There on the wall is an immense mural, maybe five feet high by over a hundred feet long. It reads:

*"Let each man pass his days in that endeavor*
*wherein his gift is greatest."*
-Propertius

What makes this mural so stunning is not only its enormous size but that it's a collage made entirely of business cards—tens of thousands of business cards from people all over the world! There are business cards of plumbers, lawyers, accountants, auditors, insurance agents, investment bankers and yes, salespeople. As you look at the massive display that stretches down the wall, you can't help but stand in awe of the sheer number of professions out there, each drawing different people to their own calling in life.

It should be no surprise that those who succeed in any job or career do so because 1) They actually enjoy their work and 2) They are good at what they do. They are successful plumbers, lawyers, accountants, auditors, insurance agents, investment bankers and salespeople because that's what they want to be and because that's where their talents lie. Question: Are you passing your days in the endeavor where your gift is the greatest?

Is a career in sales really your calling? Is this what you want to do and what you feel you are cut out to do? If your answers to these two questions are both no, it is my guess you are not doing very well right now and that you may never do very well in selling. Perhaps you are thinking:

*"This isn't what I should be doing with my life."*
*"I'm not very good at sales."*
*"I don't like talking to people."*
*"I'm not proud of what I do for a living."*
*"This is just a temporary thing until I find something better."*

With this kind of negative attitude you are doomed to fail, or at best to have a merely pedestrian career in sales. If the statements you just read reflect your stance on selling, you already have one foot out the door. Perhaps it is time to put the other foot in motion, start walking, and find another line of work. The sooner you move on the better. I'm not saying that to be mean; I'm saying that to be helpful! If you loathe what you do for a living or you don't feel you can do it very well, why would you stay? Nine out of ten people will tell you that their greatest goal in life is to be happy. If you are not happy doing what you are doing for a living, what kind of life is that? Move on! (Visit the mural in the Atlanta airport and you'll find thousands of colorful career options you may find more rewarding and to your liking.)

This is a tough lesson to deliver at this early stage of the book, but an important one. If you want to be a success in the field of selling, you have to like people, like selling and feel you are cut out for it. That is the price of admission. All others may apply for work elsewhere.

On the other hand, if you truly enjoy selling, are challenged by the role, like the freedom and opportunities the job provides and are fulfilled by the lure of the recognition and money you can earn, you are in the right place right now. You my friend hold the basic ingredients for big time success. It's now up to you to learn new skills, try new things, and watch your results, your income and your career climb to new heights. Your positive attitude will help you take positive action that will lead you toward positive results.

# Green Zone Selling

Adding to our previous work, the three most important lessons you just learned are:

» **Focus your mind and your goals on reaching the top 20 percent of the sales professionals in your company or industry. That's where 80 percent of the money is made.**

» **Selling itself is easy. Success in selling is hard. Don't think implementing one thing will make the difference. Success is more complex than that. There are no shortcuts.**

» **If you don't like selling and don't want to be in sales, get out now. If you like selling and want to be in sales, get moving...now!**

We're off to a good start in The Mind Zone, and discovering how to create the right attitude for success. And we've only just begun. The next few lessons will help mold your positive mindset even more.

# The Definition of "Work"

Joe Girard is known for being the top automotive salesperson of all time. Joe's success is unparalleled in his industry; no one even comes close to his career numbers in car sales. Joe was once asked about his secret to success. He responded:

> *"When I eat, I eat. When I sleep, I sleep.*
> *When I play, I play. When I work, I work."*

Girard went on to explain that if you want to be a top salesperson, you have to spend every minute at work *actually working*. He noticed that many of his colleagues came to work not to work but to socialize, to read the paper, snack, play on the computer, even to catch up on their sleep! Joe was different. He came to work to work. Maybe that's why in an industry of so many sub-par performers Joe Girard became a multi-millionaire.

Do you see eye-to-eye with Joe's concept of work? Some people don't. The Bureau of Labor Statistics recently reported that American workers spend as much as 30 percent of their day engaged in activities that have nothing to do with their jobs. Thirty percent! The study found that while people were supposed to be working they were instead making personal phone calls, running errands, playing on the Internet, balancing their checkbooks, reading magazines, talking about sports, taking smoke breaks and performing a host of other time-consuming tasks having nothing to do with their jobs. (My father, who had an admirable work ethic all his life, would say that: "Work is not someplace that you go, it is something that you do!")

If you want to take your sales and your success to higher levels, you need to embrace the true concept of work. Your workplace is not a social club. It is a place to work, to earn money to support yourself and your family and build your career. If you are in sync with that idea, good. If not, start to move your mind in that direction…fast.

High performers and top 20 percent producers are crystal clear on the notion of work. I have the privilege of conducting on-site visits with many superstar salespeople both as a business coach and in my research work. What do I notice? These people work! They waste little time. They don't get involved in long-winded office conversations. They aren't skipping through their day doing personal errands. They are busy! They are intentional, focused, fast-paced people making contacts, getting things accomplished, talking with customers (and making money!) from the time they arrive at work to the time they leave. (Question: If I shadowed you for a day, is that what I would see?)

Your mindset for success must absolutely accept an understanding of what work is all about—that "work" is not a noun, but a verb. Work is not someplace you go, but something you must do, do a lot of, and do well if you want to be successful.

I know you might see other salespeople around you not working much while they are at work. (As a matter of fact, some salespeople try to get away with doing as little work as possible!) It may be tempting to follow their lead, but where will it lead you? Are the people you see goofing off all day highly successful? No. Are they the superstars in your company? Of course not. People with a laissez-faire attitude about work are the bottom dwellers, the marginal salespeople, and usually the next person to be let go.

If you work eight hours a day, *work* eight hours a day. Leave personal stuff for personal time. The more work you do every day the more opportunities and customers you will find and the more money you'll make every year. Get your mind right on this lesson and maintain the right attitude toward the meaning of work. Work is where you make your money, and if you want to make more money, you have to spend more time working. Some people say: "But isn't it about working smarter, not harder?" No, it is not. People who don't like to work and are looking for excuses not to work say stupid things like that.

Top producers are top producers because they put in a lot of hours and work harder than everyone else. As a matter of fact, I recently polled 50 sales managers and asked them to identify the most recognizable trait that made their best salespeople their best salespeople. The number one answer? Work ethic.

# What's on Your Mind?

Do you have kids? If so, you'll really get the point of this lesson. If not, you were a kid at one time, so you can relate.

Suppose your young son came to you and said he was thinking of trying out for the school basketball team or your daughter said she wanted to be a doctor someday. As a good parent, what would you tell your child? Would you say: "Oh, don't waste your time, you'll never make it. There are so many other kids so much better than you. Don't even try; it's best not to disappoint yourself anyway."

Is that what you'd say? Of course not. You'd support your child with a "You go!" or a "That's fantastic!" or even an "I'm proud of you for trying. Do your best and I'll bet you'll make it!" Good parents encourage their children by giving them the confidence to stretch themselves to succeed in life.

So why don't you often encourage yourself the same way? Many salespeople—rather than pushing themselves to take chances and do things they want and need to do—hold back. They tell themselves they *can't*. For example:

> *I can't make my numbers this month.*
> *I can't find more prospects.*
> *I can't become a top producer.*

19

These are called self-limiting beliefs. You are limiting your opportunities and chances for success because of what you are telling yourself you can't do. (Remember the children's short story of *The Little Engine That Could?* The little locomotive wouldn't try to climb that steep hill because he kept telling himself he could not make it. Only until he changed his mind and beliefs—"I think I can, I think I can!"—did he try…and succeed.)

If you are game for a little eye-opening experiment, take out a piece of paper and make a list of things you have been telling yourself lately that you can't do. For example:

- I can't sell that new product
- I can't figure out our computer system
- I can't speak in front of a group of people
- I can't get out and make more sales calls
- I can't find any new customers

When you've finished, stare at each one of your self-limiting beliefs. Ask yourself: Why can't I do these things? Why are these things so impossible for me? How come other salespeople can do these things and I cannot? Why do I think this way?

You'll quickly realize that the only reason why you can't do most (if not all) of the things you've listed is because *you are telling yourself you can't.* That's it. It's you. Your own self-limiting beliefs are your biggest obstacles. You may believe in your kids, but you don't believe in yourself. You may encourage others to try and do things, but you don't encourage yourself. How you allow yourself to think may be the biggest barrier standing in your way of doing the things you want and need to be doing to become a greater success in selling. (Think about that!)

If you are ready to improve your results, stop thinking *I can't* and start thinking *I can.*

*I can deliver a presentation in front of a group of people.*
*I can find time every day for follow up phone calls.*
*I can better control my schedule and my day.*
*I can learn that new software program.*
*I can become a top producer.*

Talk about moving your mind to the Green Zone! This manner of positive thinking and optimistic self-talk is a perfect example of a salesperson "going green." Remember that your mind controls your thoughts and actions. If you let your mind think you can, then you'll try. And if you try, you have a much higher chance of succeeding than if you don't. There is real truth in the silly cliché: *Success is packaged in cans!*

# The Serenity Prayer

You are discovering in this part of the book that your mind is an amazing thing. It can be a great ally in your ability to navigate into and through the Green Zone of selling. Your beliefs and your thoughts drive your actions, and those actions create your results.

But your mind can also play tricks on you! Since two primary functions of your brain are to analyze situations and solve problems, your mind can mistakenly occupy itself with the wrong agenda. Thus we have the message behind the famous Serenity Prayer:

*God, grant me the serenity*
*to accept the things I cannot change,*
*the courage to change the things I can,*
*and the wisdom to know the difference.*

Good advice, right? How many times are salespeople preoccupied with issues, challenges and problems they cannot solve? How much time and energy do they often waste analyzing and discussing factors affecting their success that are far outside of their control?

Case in point: I spoke at a company's regional quarterly sales meeting recently. My workshop was scheduled in the afternoon from 1 to 3 pm and I wanted to sit in on the morning session of presentations and discussions to get a feel for the group. I was astonished to see how much time was spent (wasted) talking about things these people had no control over. They sat there all morning and discussed the global economy, new government regulations, what the competition was up to, corporate forecasts, the financial outlook for the next few fiscal quarters—they actually spent almost fifteen minutes debating whether their company logo was "catchy" enough!

What should this team of 20 sales professionals been doing while they had the rare luxury of being together for three hours that morning?

- Analyzing new market opportunities
- Sharing successful selling strategies
- Discussing best practices for landing appointments
- Practicing their phone and face-to-face selling skills
- Debating and discovering their company strengths
- Finding ways to handle customer concerns and objections
- Planning new sales campaigns for the weeks ahead

Instead, they wasted a fantastic networking and learning opportunity to make positive progress toward the *things they can change.* (Perhaps they lacked the wisdom to know the difference?)

Make sure you are not making the same mistake with your valuable time, energy and amazing brain. Focus on the things you can control. Have the wisdom to know the difference between what you can affect…and what you can't. Every day at work, be mindful of this.

There are hundreds of things you cannot control or change. You have no control over the nation's economy, government regulations or your company's direction. You have no say in your competitor's pricing, the stock market or inclement weather. Spend no time obsessing about these things. Let none of them occupy a second of your attention or a minute of your conversations at work. Instead, invest your valuable and limited time and energy focused on things within your control.

The next time you encounter a problem, situation, bad news or changes affecting your business, ask yourself one question: *Can I do something about it?* If the answer is no, leave it. Worrying, fretting, even fixating over circumstances you cannot control or change gets in the way of what you are supposed to be doing that day—running your business and making sales. Have the wisdom to focus your time, energy and talents instead on what you *can* control: things within your scope of influence. What can you control?

- Your attitude and outlook
- Your work schedule
- Your goals and plans
- How you spend your time
- The number of sales contacts you make
- How you take care of your customers

# Green Zone Selling

Here's a summary of the last three lessons:

» **Work is not someplace you go, it is something you do. Spend your work time working. You'll get more done every day and make more money every year.**

» **Beware of self-limiting beliefs. You will believe the things your mind tells you to believe. Stop telling yourself you can't do things. Start telling yourself you can.**

» **Be smart enough to recognize the things you cannot change and leave them alone. Focus instead on the things you can control...and take action!**

Are you starting to see what the Green Zone is all about? Many people think that selling is all about scripts, presentations and skills. While all these are important, it first takes the right *mindset* to know how to apply them.

There are three more lessons in Part One. They are important ones.

# Leave the Herd Behind

What Vilfredo Pareto taught us a few lessons back is that 20 percent of the salespeople in your industry close 80 percent of the sales and make 80 percent of the money. If you want to be in that top 20 percent (which you do) you'd be smart to run with the leaders of the pack. "You become the company you keep," the old saying goes. If you hang around with the bottom 80 percent of the salespeople in your office or company, you will soon become just like them (or if you are already just like them, stay like them).

Let's illustrate this point. Say for example you wanted to lose some weight and get in better shape. Suppose there is a group of people you know who are very fit and trim. They look fantastic! They exercise regularly, play energizing games of basketball at lunchtime and sometimes take evening walks or runs together after work. They watch what they eat and encourage and support each other's healthy living habits. By contrast, there is also a group of people you know who are overweight and lazy. They order in pizza for lunch and drink sodas all day long. They spend their time in the evenings on the sofa watching TV and smoking cigarettes. Now, if you were really serious about getting in better shape, with which group of friends do you think you'd have a better chance of success?

You get my point; *you become the company you keep.* This rings true at work as well. If you keep company with marginal salespeople who produce marginal results or are struggling or complaining a lot, you could eventually become one of them—a complaining, struggling, marginal salesperson.

You must surround yourself with successful people if you plan to be a success. Winners will lift you up...and losers will drag you down. Winners will energize you with their ideas, skills, and positive outlooks. Losers will contaminate you with their problems, lackadaisical attitudes and excuses for poor performance.

Take a look around you at the company you now keep. Are these people winners? We just talked about the importance of change and here is where you may need to make your first change. I have seen how the bottom 80 percent work, and so have you:

- They come to work late and often slip out early
- They don't have a plan for their day; they just react
- They spend their time doing the least important things
- They socialize a lot at work and play around on the computer
- They gripe a lot and make excuses for their lack of results

Does this sound like anyone you associate with at work? In your climb to reach the top 20 percent (or in your efforts to stay in that top 20 percent) you need to leave them far behind. This may be difficult. These folks might be your friends and they may be nice people. But they are holding you back from finding more sales and making more money...and you know it. The lesson here is simple: Hang with successful people if you want to become a success. They will show you how it's done.

# Affirming Your Beliefs

An "affirmation" is defined as positive self-talk. By continually repeating positive messages aloud, you condition your mind to a positive mental state: a way of optimistic brainwashing, if you will.

Think about a golfer eying a ten foot putt to win the championship. If he says: "I'm going to blow this shot," he'll likely miss the hole. Great golfers know that golf is both a physical and mental game. Positive self-talk leads to a better chance of positive results. It does not *guarantee* positive results, but it does lead to a better chance of achieving them.

Like golf, selling is both a physical and a mental game. Work on your mental game with more positive self-talk and you will improve your results. Read the following aloud: (Don't just think it, say it out loud!)

> *I like my job.*
> *I am a good at what I do.*
> *I am on my way to success!*

Doesn't that sound empowering? Now imagine reciting this five second exercise just three times each day; on the way to work, at lunch, and on the way home. In the course of a month, you'd speak this affirmation around 60 times. Over a year you'd affirm your belief more than 700 times; in five years, 3,500 times. If you *really* like being in sales and you *really* think you are good at what you do and you *really* intend to capitalize on each day's opportunities to become an even greater success, this affirmation, repeated continually, will help create a state of mind for success. Again:

> *I like my job.*
> *I am good at what I do.*
> *I am on my way to success!*

Hundreds of outstanding books have been researched and written about this very topic. Along with the aforementioned *Think and Grow Rich* by Napoleon Hill, there's *The Power of Positive Thinking* by Norman Vincent Peale and *The Secret* by Rhonda Byrne. These outstanding works confirm the undeniable fact you learned earlier—that how you think and what you say form the basis for how you act. And as we now know, how you act and what you do is the foundation for the results you achieve.

Negative self-talk leads to non-action. Why pick up the phone and call that potential customer if you tell yourself he won't be interested in talking to you? Why follow up with a prospect if you believe she has already made a decision to buy elsewhere? Why make sales calls on clients if you've already told yourself it will be a waste of time? Why introduce yourself to a new prospect if you are embarrassed about what you do for a living?

Positive self-talk leads to proactive, positive action which will lead you to more opportunities, more sales, more money, and more positive results. (I call this The Cycle of Sales Success.) On the other hand, negative self-talk leads to...well...let's see:

*"Here we go again. Another day in this crappy place."*
*"There's no sense in making calls. It's*
*Monday and everybody's busy."*
*"I'm not going to run this ad. It will be a waste of money."*
*"I'll follow up on this lead, but it will probably be worthless."*
*"I'll be lucky if I can get anything accomplished today!"*

I can only imagine the kind of day this salesperson is going to have! His negative self-talk is his own worst enemy. He isn't struggling because of problems with his product, price, service levels, or competition. He just can't get out of his own negative way!

By contrast, here's an example of how a Green Zone salesperson starts his or her day with positive self-talk:

*"This is going to be a productive day for me."*
*"I need to make some calls. I'll catch somebody in right now."*
*"I am going to run this ad and get some new customers."*
*"I'll bet if I follow up on these leads I'll land at least one sale."*
*"Let's see how much I can get done today!"*

Your first reaction to this lesson might be: "Come on; do you really think this positive self-talk stuff will make a difference?" Yes, I do. I not only think it will make a difference, I know it. I have trained and coached many salespeople to re-program their thoughts and words to positive affirmations and I have seen the difference it makes not just in their attitudes but in their actions, their results and their incomes along the way.

We'll delve more deeply into this later on, but for now start to tune your mind to a more positive, optimistic wavelength. This will be the basis necessary for exploring Part Two of this book. Indulge me one more time:

> *I like my job.*
> *I am good at what I do.*
> *I am on my way to success!*

# Get Started and Don't Give Up!

We sometimes think being good at selling is an innate ability. "You either have it or you don't," many people say. But success in selling can be as much about *tenacity* as it is about talent. Those who succeed in selling bring an attitude of persistence and dogged determination to what they do. In short, they have the ability to get things started and not give up. Case in point:

There's a training program I deliver called "The 90-Day Blitz." It is a sales process designed for business-to-business sales professionals. Followed through to completion, I guarantee every salesperson participating in the program will land at least two new high-quality, long-term business clients in less than 90 days. The program involves six steps:

1.  Identify 20 potential prospects.
2.  Send each prospect a targeted letter introducing yourself and your company's products or services.

3. Follow up in five days with a phone call asking for a brief 15-minute appointment.
4. Hold the appointment meeting and discover if there is an interest and opportunity with the client.
5. Mail a thank-you letter along with your proposal information.
6. Follow up with a phone call in five days asking for a decision.

All in all, it is a simple, straightforward process with supplied scripts, letters, tracking charts and everything the salesperson needs to execute the blitz. It begins with a four-hour interactive workshop and helpful advice on how to initiate the program literally the very next day. It also takes into account capture and conversion rates; not every prospect they identify will be interested and not everyone initially interested will become a customer. Everything is there; nothing is left to chance.

I recently conducted another session of "The 90-Day Blitz" for a group of 15 salespeople at a bank. Since the program involves structured coaching via conference calls and progress reporting every two weeks during the 90-day time frame, I tracked the group's success at each stage. I share this information with you because this group is typical of most every group I have trained. Here are their results:

| | |
|---|---|
| # of participants in the program = | 15 |
| # of participants gathering 20 names of prospects = | 9 |
| # of participants sending out the introductory letter = | 7 |
| # of participants making the follow up calls = | 7 |
| # of participants holding appointment meetings = | 6 |
| # of participants sending out follow up letters = | 6 |
| # of participants making follow up phone calls = | 3 |
| # of participants landing two new clients = | 3 |

Notice anything peculiar? Most of the fallout happens early

in the process. Of 15 participants, six never even bothered to get started. Another two got the names but never sent out the first letter. We lost over half of the group in the first two steps of the program. Of the three participants who followed the plan through to the finish, all achieved their goal and reaped the rewards of two new client relationships and more sales.

The Perato Principle triumphs again. Three out of 15 people (20 percent) succeeded because three of 15 had the tenacity to get started immediately and follow the plan through to completion. Fifteen participants had the same plan, the same coaching, the same letters, scripts, and the same follow up assistance. But six never even got started and only three had the gumption to go the distance.

Success in selling is often about getting started and staying with the plan all the way through. It's not about bailing out, giving up, getting distracted, or letting good opportunities get away. All 15 salespeople at the bank were excited to be in the program and all of them wanted more customers, more business and more money. What differentiated the three who succeeded from the 12 who didn't was not their desire or their skills or their training. It was their willingness to start something positive and see it all the way through. Not everyone can do this. Can you?

How many great sales strategies have you not acted upon? How many seminars have you walked away from with good ideas that you never implemented? How many new marketing plans have you undertaken...and then gave up on or let fall by the wayside?

We are now concluding The Mind Zone of this book. A great deal of your success from here on will come from the ideas and actions you implement and follow through to completion. This has to be your way of thinking. Successful salespeople are successful because they are willing to do the things unsuccessful salespeople won't do. Be one of those successful salespeople— start to finish!

31

# Green Zone Selling

Let's review the final lessons in Part One: The Mind Zone

» **For you to be counted among the top salespeople in your company or industry, you need to leave the herd behind. Associate only with successful salespeople at work and you will learn much from their winning ways.**

» **Positive affirmations are a powerful way to condition your mind for success. Think and say positive things out loud and you will take more positive action, which will lead you to more positive results.**

» **Success in selling is as much about *tenacity* as it is talent. Those who succeed bring an attitude of persistence and determination to what they do. They have the mindset to get things started... and not give up.**

# Part Two
## The Time Zone

# Time is _____

Do you remember your very first job? It was probably like mine, a teenage hourly wage job. I made ice cream cones at the local Dairy Queen for $1 an hour (whoopee!) I had a clear understanding of what my time was worth. If I worked five hours that day, I made five bucks. If I worked 30 hours a week, I'd earn $30. Remember your first job?

Now that you are in sales and working on commission, perhaps you've lost sight of the hourly value of your time. You most likely don't punch a time clock or keep close track of exactly how many hours you work in a given week. In any event, just like your first job, you are transacting a trade; you are trading your time for money.

To appreciate the exact value your time, divide what you earn by the hours you work. For example, if Jan works 160 hours this month (40 hours a week for four weeks) and earns $3,000 in sales commissions, her time is worth $18.75 an hour. If Joe works the same schedule of 160 hours and earns $13,000 in commissions, his time is worth $81.25 an hour. Do this experiment for yourself right now. Take what you earned last month in commission income and divide it by how many hours you worked. That's your current hourly wage. (Interesting, isn't it?)

Understanding the hourly value of your time makes you think differently about how you spend it. Let's suppose after doing this calculation you discover your time is worth $60 an hour. Knowing this number helps put into perspective where you are investing your time in productive, profitable Green Zone activities and where you are wasting your time in non-productive, non-profitable activities. If you stop in the break room and chat with another co-worker for just 15 minutes about some ball game or TV show, that conversation "cost" you $15. Was that really worth it? How about searching for funny videos on the Internet for 20 minutes. You just "spent" 20 bucks. Taking off today for an hour to get a hair cut? That'll be $60 please (plus the cost of the haircut.)

Becoming more consciously aware of the value of your time on an hourly basis and how you are spending that time will help you recognize whether you are investing it wisely or wasting it foolishly. "Time is money" is a common saying, but for you as a commissioned salesperson who does not rely on a guaranteed paycheck, time truly *is* money. When you spend your time in the right places doing the right things, you get more of the right things accomplished and make more money. Simple enough to say; harder than you think to do. This part of the book will help you change how you look at your day and invest your valuable time…hopefully forever.

# Functioning in the Green Zone

You know your job better than I do, so let me ask you two questions about it:

> *What are the most productive things*
> *you can do with your time?*

> *What are the least productive things*
> *you can do with your time?*

If you can answer these two questions, you already grasp the concept of this lesson. Since you are trading one valuable commodity (time) for another (money) a critical key to your success is making the right trade. Top producing salespeople distinguish themselves from average producers by how they spend (or trade) their time every day. Because they invest more of their time in high-profit, highly-productive activities, they land more sales and make more money than everyone else. (Read that sentence again; it is important to this lesson and to how you spend your time from here on.)

One salesperson I know is a perfect example of this principle in practice. When I first met Rick about five years ago, he was a top producing salesman earning about $300,000 a year. He worked around 50 hours a week—sometimes a little more, sometimes a little less—and took off four weeks a year for personal time and family vacations. If we apply our previous "time is money" lesson here, Rick's hourly wage was $125 an hour.

Then one day, Rick had an epiphany moment. While waiting to see his doctor for an annual physical, Rick realized his time (at $125 an hour) was worth as much as or more than his doctor! He observed that the doctor's assistant scheduled his appointment for that day, a receptionist checked him in, a nurse took his vital signs, and there he was sitting in a ready room to see a doctor with whom he might spend ten minutes. Rick's doctor wasn't slighting his patients—he was a business professional who understood the value of his time. He invested his time doing the highest impact, highest profit activities (seeing patients, treating illnesses and prescribing medicines) and left the rest for others to do.

Rick's appreciation of his time changed forever that day. He went back to work and made a list of the activities that represented the highest and best use of his time. He made a second list of the things that occupied a lot of his time, yet led to little or no tangible or profitable results. He typed up the list and stuck it in his day planner. To my understanding, Rick uses that list to this day, and his results and income have only increased because of it.

There's no reason why you can't enjoy the same results Rick enjoys, and it will start with creating that list. Take out a sheet of paper and make two columns. On one side, label the column "High Payoff" and record the activities that represent the highest and best use of your time. Label the other column "Low Payoff" and write down the activities that represent low or no profit activities. Type up your list, read it over, and keep it somewhere you'll see it every day. Use the lists as a guide for how and where you invest your time from here onward. Then…

# Learn to Let Go

There are things in your job you should not be doing, and there are things you should get or pay others to do for you. Do you agree with that? If so, skip over the next paragraph and my lecture on this subject. If not, this little bit of coaching is for you:

In spending three decades exposed to thousands of salespeople, I've concluded most of them are "control freaks." Because they won't let or don't trust others to help them, they burden themselves with so many non-productive, non-profitable, non-sales tasks. Maybe being unwilling to delegate is a means of "feeling" busy when they are not. Or perhaps they were taught: "If you want something done right you have to do it yourself!" Whatever the reason, many salespeople who refuse to hand off and release themselves of activities that are not worth their time earn far less money than they should. Only until they face-down this fact and learn to let go do they move forward.

Let's get to work on the "Low Payoff" list you created earlier. First, look for activities that are supposed to be done by others. Are you spending your time doing other people's jobs for them? Why? Stop it today! Every minute you invest doing someone else's job is a minute you lose to do your own job. Talk to them, train the, fire them, whatever. If they are employed and paid to do certain things, let them do those things so you don't have to. Here's the bottom line: *When you stop doing what you shouldn't be doing, you will have the time to start doing more of the things you should be doing.*

Second, look for activities you can "hire out." Rick's doctor hired out a number of tasks at rates much lower than the value of his time. You can too. Should you bring on board an assistant? Can you farm out some tasks to others at an hourly or per-project rate? Before you say that can't be done in your line of business, consider a few of these examples I have seen other salespeople do:

- Hire a web designer to build or update your website
- Hire your son or daughter to seal, stamp and send out your monthly marketing mailings
- Hire your spouse to update your computer system
- Hire the teenage neighbor kid to design your Facebook page
- Hire a temp to develop a customer database CRM system and set up your entire client contact program
- Hire a marketing major at a local college to create your new personal brochure or business card
- Hire a service to answer your phone when you are on sales calls or out of town traveling

Paying for most all of these tasks will cost you less than your hourly wage. That frees up your time to focus on the High Payoff activities that will bring you more sales.

Third, make a final scan of the Low Payoff list and draw a line through things that you know you simply should not be doing with your time. If it doesn't make sense for you to do these things and they are not someone else's job and you don't think you should pay someone else to handle them, why would you do them at all?

When you are finished with this exercise, you'll look at your time and your job quite differently. I have done this exercise myself, and I have helped others do it. It is amazing. Try it now before you go any further. It could be a game-changer for you.

# Green Zone Selling

Welcome to the Time Zone! Remember:

» **Time is money. Every day you trade one valuable commodity (time) for another (money). Understand clearly the dollar value of what your time is actually worth.**

» **Learn to separate your High Payoff activities from Low Payoff activities. Be aware of the best and most productive places to spend your time. More time invested in High Payoff activities will quickly increase your income.**

» **Learn to let go! Delegate where you can and allow others to do their jobs. Look to "hire out" activities that can be done by other people at an hourly wage less than yours.**

Top salespeople who earn enormous amounts of money are masters of time. Everyone has the same 24 hours a day. It's how you use them that counts!

# Making Forward Progress

Comedian Larry the Cable Guy says: "Get 'er done!" A funny punch line for a stand-up bit, but also incredibly applicable advice when it comes to selling.

Your goal every day is to make *forward progress*. This Green Zone way of thinking—a conscious awareness of getting things done—is what drives the days and careers of highly-successful salespeople. And there is no better tool for this task than the well-established—but often mis-applied—To-Do List.

I know you've heard about To-Do Lists; you may already use this tool from time to time or even every day. But do you know how really great To-Do Lists actually work? Here are a few things most salespeople have never learned about how to build and use a To-Do List:

1. A To-Do List is a list of things you will get done today. Notice I did not say it was a list of things you'd like to get done or wish you could get done sometime this week. It is a list of things you *will* get done *today*. Approaching your To-Do List in this technique creates a heightened sense of urgency and changes how you plan your day and how you work with your time.

2. The best To-Do Lists contain one activity for each hour of work. If you are planning to work five hours that day, your To-Do List should show no more than five activities. If you are going to put in an eight hour day, eight activities max. It makes no sense to overload your list with 15 or 20 things. You know you won't get all that stuff done in a single day, so why think you are going to? You'll do nothing but create a life of frustration for yourself. A good To-Do List accounts for the outside world: interruptions, emergencies, surprise sales opportunities, and more. Make sure you leave time

41

in your schedule for real life by not letting too many activities on your list monopolize your time for the entire day.

3.  Some people design their To-Do Lists first thing in the morning while others prefer to construct their lists the night before. Whatever works for you is fine. Just remember: never start your day without your list completed. Don't answer a call, don't read your email and don't go to a meeting until your daily "road map" is done. Make this a routine practice, as consistent and automatic as the morning habit of brushing your teeth.

4.  Once you have drafted your list of things to do, rank that list in order of execution. Place a number 1 by the first thing you will do that day, a 2 by the second activity and so on. Prioritizing your day this way will allow you to move quickly from task to task without reviewing your list again and again to decide what you should do next. However…

5.  As you prioritize your list, be sure to place the important "High Payoff" activities first. Many salespeople take the attitude of: "Well, I'll just get a lot of little things off my desk, and when those get done I'll tackle the big projects and important tasks." Major mistake. This approach of flip-flopping the high priorities in your business with lower priorities will slow down your forward progress, maybe even stall it completely. Tackle important High Payoff activities first in the morning—the things that move your business forward—and leave the little stuff that's not as crucial for later in the day. Your 1-2-3 priority ranking should go from top to bottom in importance to your sales objectives and goals, not in

order of how easy the activities are to complete. Notice how this is illustrated in the following example:

| | |
|---|---|
| 4 | Work on Sullivan presentation |
| 6 | Call back Stan in Accounting |
| 1 | Follow up lead on Mr. Reynolds |
| 3 | Set up appointments for next week |
| 5 | Go through mailbox |
| 2 | Send out proposal to Delaney |
| 7 | Update database with new names |
| 8 | Read new product guidelines |

6. Use your To-Do List as a real-time road map throughout the day. Keep it with you, keep it in plain sight, and review it often. Remember that your list isn't *everything* you're going to do that day, just the things that absolutely need to get done. You'll still answer your phone, read your emails, hold conversations and (hopefully) enjoy some walk-in or call-in business. That stuff happens every day, and you don't need to put "answer my phone" or "read emails" on your list to remember to pick up your phone or check your emails.

7. As you progress through your day, draw a bold line through the activity on your list when it is completed. This little step adds a feeling of personal accomplishment to your day, puts the completed task in the past and out of your mind, and allows you to concentrate on the next one immediately. Your mission is to finish your To-Do List by the end of the day, not just a few things on the list, but the entire list. Don't think that's impossible because it's not. Top producers do it all the time.

8. Stay in focus! A lot of salespeople start their day with a To-Do List...and quickly give up on it. At the first

interruption or after responding to an unexpected customer call or business emergency they say, "Oh well, today is shot!" and abandon their plan. Don't do this! Yes, you'll have interruptions and yes, there will be calls and emergencies. Take care of them and return back to your list as soon as possible. (If you don't feel you can do this, save yourself the time and don't even bother to build a To-Do List in the first place. If you are going to build a plan for your day but not follow it, you might as well have no plan for your day at all.)

9. At the end of your day, look at your list. Did you get everything done? If the answer is no, ask yourself why. Did you not follow your plan? Did you allow yourself to get sidetracked? (Notice I said "allow.") Did you fill your day with busy work, co-worker conversations and personal errands? Analyze what is broken in your ability to follow your plan, find solutions, and fix it fast. The longer you permit yourself to be overly-reactive and get distracted, the harder it will be to get the things you need to get done actually done.

10. At the end of the day, if you achieved everything on your To-Do List, good for you! What a terrific, productive day! Reward yourself for your effort and commitment. Feel good about what you achieved. Go home and enjoy a wonderful evening knowing your business is on track and moving forward in the right direction.

Set a serious goal to make forward progress in your day, every day. Manage your time from a written plan—a To-Do List. Prioritize your tasks from most important and profitable to least. Stay focused, stay on task, and *get things done.*

# Important Versus Impulsive

I have had the privilege of personally coaching more than 100 sales professionals one-on-one over the last 15 years. When I start working with someone in a coaching relationship, I always ask this question: "What are the three things I can help you with the most?"

On nearly every occasion, one of the items the person mentions he or she needs help with is time management. This never surprises me. The ability to manage time is perhaps the greatest challenge every salesperson—perhaps every person—wrestles with every day. (By the way, there are more than 100,000 books listed online at Amazon.com right now that address "time management.")

I tell my coaching student that I can help him or her with better time management, but to do so, he or she has to come to grips with one undeniable fact:

*Everything is not important.*

We want to think that everything we do is important. It is not. Every meeting you are asked to attend is not important. Every email you get is not important. Every phone call you receive is not important. It's true that some meetings, emails and phone calls are important; it is equally true that many are not. (If you are often challenged throughout the day with decisions about what you should be doing next, or if you find your momentum disrupted constantly by interruptions, this may be a great lesson for you!)

We've already discovered that you have to be capable of making the right decisions about doing the right things with your time. To accomplish that, you must define the difference between things in your job that are *important* and those that are *impulsive*.

Let me illustrate. I was in Dallas, Texas, and scheduled to

speak at a sales conference the following day. When I checked into my hotel and unpacked, I noticed a weird stain on my dress shirt. There was a big mall adjacent to the hotel, so I strolled across to the parking lot to go shopping. I walked into a well-known department store, located the men's section, found a shirt and proceeded to the check-out station.

"Did you find everything okay?" asked the young saleswoman. "Yes, just this shirt please," I replied. As she began ringing up my purchase, the phone rang on the table behind her. "Excuse me," she said, and answered the phone.

I am not a rude consumer, nor was I in a big hurry, but I took notice of what was happening. The call was obviously from another employee looking for some kind of product code or item number or something. The conversation lasted about one minute. She hung up the phone, came back to the register and said, "All right, let's get you finished up."

"Can I ask you something?" I said. "Sure," she replied. I leaned forward, smiled and said, "Why did you answer that phone?" The young woman was taken aback. She looked at me completely puzzled for a moment and then said something I will never forget: "Well…it might have been a customer!"

What was the most important thing going on in her world at that moment in time? It was me, *a customer*, standing three feet away with money in hand to buy a product. Her company spends millions of dollars in advertising and marketing trying to get people like me to shop in their stores. There I was, fulfilling the mission! And I was rewarded by being placed "on hold" while she focused on a ringing telephone. She made the wrong choice that day; she tended to what was impulsive (a ringing telephone) instead of what was important (a paying customer).

Back to you. How many times have you let this happen in your day? How often do you place important and potentially money-making tasks and activities on the back burner so you can tend to impulsive things like reading your email the second it comes in? You realize that you should be making sales calls, but instead you organize your files. You know you need to follow up on prospects and leads you have from last week, but you choose to look at a web site, make copies, or stop and answer your phone every time it rings.

Why does this happen to so many salespeople? It happens for one very basic reason: it's easier. Impulsive activities are always easier to do than important activities, and many salespeople choose to take the easy road.

If you are like most salespeople and the challenge of time management is a daily dilemma, take particular note of the lesson in front of you right now. Start to look at things that pop up in your workday as falling into one of two categories: important or impulsive. Before you respond to something, ask yourself: "Is reacting to this important to me and my business? Does it contribute to my priorities, objectives and sales goals? If so, stop everything and do it now—it's important. Everything else is just impulsive. You can spend an entire day buried in impulsive activities, feel very busy, and when the day is done get nothing meaningful or profitable accomplished.

Like many of my coaching students have learned, the more time and energy you invest in the *important* activities, the more real work you'll get done every day. But it's hard. It's hard to ignore that ringing phone, that vibrating text message or that email "ding" sound on your computer. Just remember that every time you stop important activities for impulsive activities, your business takes a back-step, your attention is derailed, and your energies are diverted in the wrong direction.

If success in selling requires you to exercise good time management practices, one of those practices is staying focused on tasks that are important, not purely impulsive. Remember: *Everything is not important.* The more you can stay on track and on purpose in how you control your time and attention throughout the day, the greater number of really important things you will accomplish.

*Douglas Smith*

# A Day with Dollar Signs

If I have convinced you by now how important it is to run your day from a To-Do List and how staying focused on High Payoff activities will impact your results, then you'll love this next little "bonus" idea. It was given to me by a top sales professional many years ago. I like it so much I teach it in my time management workshops for salespeople and use it in my own business to this day. It is simple and it is brilliant. (It is simply brilliant!)

We've already learned about building a To-Do List every day and ranking the order of execution from start to finish, right? Here's the add-on idea: Scan your list one more time before you start working and place a dollar sign ($) next to those activities that have a high potential of *directly* creating an income opportunity for you that day. Just like *everything* is not important, everything you do does not make you money. Using our previous To-Do List example, here's what that might look like:

| | | |
|---|---|---|
| 4 | Work on Sullivan presentation | $ |
| 6 | Call back Stan in Accounting | |
| 1 | Follow up lead on Mr. Reynolds | $ |
| 3 | Set up appointments for next week | $ |
| 5 | Go through mailbox | |
| 2 | Send out proposal to Delaney | $ |
| 7 | Update database with new names | |
| 8 | Read new product guidelines | |

This salesperson has eight activities planned for the day that she needs to get done, all important to her business. On the left, she has ranked them in order of execution from one through eight, in her sequence of execution. Now, check out her dollar signs ($) in the right column. Four of the eight activities are *directly* linked to potential sales and commission opportunities. (Notice these are also the first four things she plans to do that day. Pretty smart salesperson!) It's not that the other four tasks are unimportant. She needs to call Stan back in the Accounting Department, she needs to go through her mailbox, update her database and read those new product guidelines. It's just that those activities are not *directly* related to an income opportunity that day and therefore do not warrant dollar signs.

A day with more dollar signs means a day with more potential to make more money. A day with few or no dollar signs indicates a day of busy work and little or no income opportunities. What kind of day would you rather have?

If one of your goals is to increase your income, I highly recommend adding this step to your To-Do List. You'll start to see how much of your day is *directly* linked to income generating activities. In a short while, you'll learn to trade more of your valuable time for more money-making activities every day—and that's a very good trade.

# Green Zone Selling

As you learn how to better manage your time, you'll learn how to get more done and make more money.

» **A To-Do List is the single, best time management tool ever invented. Control your time by incorporating a To-Do List into your routine every day.**

» **Everything is not important. Separate tasks that crop up in your day into "impulsive" or "important." Avoid the tendency to jump on impulsive activities all day long.**

» **Want to focus on making more money every day? Place a dollar sign ($) next to every item on your To-Do List that directly relates to an income opportunity. You'll see how much of your day is actually spent making money!**

There are three more lessons in Part Two that will help you get the most out of your single greatest asset: your time.

# The 25 Percent Rule

Nearly every salesperson who is not making enough money is not making enough sales contacts. From my research, the average-performing salesperson spends from 5 percent to 10 percent of his or her time "prospecting" for new business while the typical top producer invests over twice that amount engaged in prospecting, marketing, networking, and follow-up activities. (See a pattern here?)

Want more sales? As a fundamental rule, you should allocate a minimum of 25 percent of your time engaged in some form of proactive prospecting. That means if you work a typical eight hour day and 40 hour week, you should invest, on average, two hours a day and ten hours a week looking for new customers and more sales. If that's what you are doing now, you likely have the results to show for it. If that's not what you are doing now, it is likely you are not closing enough sales.

First, let's define prospecting. Prospecting is what you do to *find* a customer. It's not answering questions, writing up contracts or servicing your existing customer's accounts. Prospecting is all about finding the *next* customer and *another* sales opportunity. Common prospecting activities for many salespeople include:

- Making out-bound phone calls
- Trying to set up new appointments
- Mailing out letters, flyers, offers and marketing materials
- Placing ads
- Sending out solicitation emails
- Attending networking functions
- Following up on leads
- Contacting customers about repeat business
- Phoning good clients and asking for their referrals

Are you investing at least 25 percent of your time each

day engaged in these types of activities? You should be. Those salespeople who spend more time looking for more customers and more sales always (repeat: always) find more customers and make more sales.

Second, let's talk about *planning* to prospect. How does prospecting fit into your daily routine? Is it an *important* activity? If you view prospecting as a "left-over time" activity or a dreaded chore, you'll rarely if ever find time to do it. Prospecting is important to your sales growth and needs to be a *priority* on your To-Do List. Perhaps you have heard of terms like Time Blocking, Time Mapping, or as I like to teach it: Time Framing. Essentially, this is the practice of protecting pieces of time for important things in your job—like prospecting. For example, if you worked a 40-hour week and were to commit 25 percent of your time for prospecting activities on a weekly basis, you could:

- Frame two hours each day on your calendar, from 10 am to noon, as time dedicated for your prospecting activities or…
- Frame four hours on Monday afternoon, three hours on Wednesday afternoon and three hours on Friday afternoon for prospecting or…
- Frame all day Tuesday and all of Thursday morning for prospecting

Try out this concept. Work it however it works for you. Just be sure at least 25 percent of your time is continuously allocated to some method of prospecting. This is how top-producing salespeople ensure their important prospecting activities get done…and keep getting done week after week and month after month. There is little argument for the statement that prospecting is the Highest Yield activity that drives new customers and more sales opportunities in the door. And above everything else, isn't that what you, *as a salesperson*, are there to do?

# A Case for Discipline

Several years ago I heard about a sales manager in Minnesota who led a very successful team of top producers. They were the number one branch in their company of more than 50 offices and commanded the biggest market share of business in the region. Always looking for more success stories to share with my clients, I called and asked for a personal interview with the office sales manager, Michael, who graciously agreed.

"The fundamental key to our success here is discipline," Michael told me. "Selling itself is a discipline, and I've learned that those who do well in sales are extremely disciplined individuals. I hire only ex-military men and women and former college athletes."

Wow. That caught my attention. He hired *only* ex-military people and former college athletes? I asked him how he could do that. "I just do," he replied. "It's my office and I can hire who I want and that's who I hire." Michael went on to say: "These people have learned the importance of discipline and have it deeply engrained in them. They come to me with no experience in selling and no knowledge of our products or our business. But knowledge can be taught and experience is over-rated. Discipline is a character trait. Former military people and college athletes have it. I can't teach discipline; you either own it or you don't. That single trait makes or breaks anyone in sales. And here it makes people very successful and very wealthy."

While you may not agree with Michael's employment practices, you can't argue his reasoning. He's right. *Discipline is a central trait that drives a salesperson's success.*

As you develop your personal discipline, you improve your image as a sales professional, your opportunities for business, and your results. Discipline itself is not complicated. It's made up of simple things you demonstrate every day in many simple ways, like:

- Coming to work on time
- Being prompt for meetings, appointments, webinars and conference calls
- Creating a To-Do List each morning…and following it
- Sending a thank-you card after every customer appointment
- Making weekly sales calls and visits to existing clients
- Filling out your monthly sales reports and submitting them on time
- Delivering to people the things you promise them within the time frames you have promised

The more I think about this sales manager's philosophy, the more I see his point. Most (if not all) of the best and richest salespeople I have ever met are very disciplined individuals. They are among the first to arrive at work. They have developed effective work flows and customer contact systems. They build annual business plans, leads tracking charts and client databases. They move through their day with purpose. *They are disciplined.*

To be disciplined means to be intentional and organized. Organization creates efficiency. Efficiency creates more time. Having more time available means you can make more customer contacts, return phone calls faster and follow up on leads and new opportunities more frequently. And all of that means more sales and more money. (Again we have the Green Zone of success!)

This would be a good time for another self-assessment. If you could assign yourself a report card type "grade" on discipline, what would it be?

A = I am incredibly disciplined in how I run my business
B = I am mostly disciplined in how I run my business
C = I am somewhat disciplined, somewhat not
D = I am not at all disciplined in how I run my business
F = I am so screwed up I have no idea what I am doing next

If you graded yourself anything less than a B in the assessment above, you must decide that from here on you will force yourself to operate in a more disciplined manner.

1. You will be on time for work every day.
2. You will be prompt for team meetings, conference calls and webinars.
3. You will submit your reports when they are due.
4. You will run your day from a To-Do List.
5. You will track your leads and sources of business.
6. You will follow up with every potential prospect.
7. You will follow through on all of your promises.

That's what being "disciplined" is all about, and it will make an enormous difference in how people see you and the new results you will achieve. (Just imagine what moving from one grade up to the next would do for your professional image and sales results!)

Discipline, as Michael the sales manager noted, cannot be taught. There are no classes to take or books that can be read that will "make" you a more disciplined salesperson. It's a choice. From here on, what's your choice going to be?

# The Right People

In a few moments you'll be entering the third part of this book: The Contact Zone. There you'll learn all sorts of great new selling skills and approaches to use when you are on the phone or face-to-face with your customers. But before we get there, let's go here:

> *Success in selling*
> *is about spending the right amount of time*
> *with the right people*
> *delivering the right message.*

We'll get to the "right message" piece in the next series. For now, let's stay with the first point of this advice as it relates to your time.

There are three types and only three types of customers in the world: those that will buy, those that might buy, and those that will not buy. You should spend 75 percent of your prospecting time with the first group of people, 25 percent with the second and zero percent with the third. For you to sell something, the customer has to be ready and able to buy it. Therefore, *who* you spend your valuable prospecting time with can mean the difference between success and starvation.

High performing salespeople are in tune with this practice and line of thinking. If a customer can't buy, doesn't want to buy, isn't ready to buy or can't afford to buy, *he is not a customer!* Your first objective in sizing up a prospect is to determine as quickly as you can if he or she is a potential customer or not. At the risk of being ridiculously obvious: *Wasting your time with non-customers is nonsense.*

I made this last comment not long ago at one of my sales seminars. Afterwards, a woman in attendance came up to me and said she disagreed. "I'll work with a lot of people that I know aren't real customers," she confessed. "Even though I know they're probably never going to buy, at least I feel like I'm busy and not just sitting around." I hope you are as floored with her remarks as I was. In her mind, she was justifying the fact she was totally wasting her time with people who she knew were never going to buy. Instead of investing her time looking for and landing real customers, she was bogging down her day with…well…nonsense. (I wonder where she is bagging groceries these days.)

When you are selling in the Green Zone you are spending time with the right people—people who have the green (money!) and are ready to buy (go!) Wasting your time with lookie-lous, shoppers and posers is costing you time which is costing you money—maybe lots of money. If you are doing that now, stop. If you aren't doing that, good for you. Never start.

Just like our earlier lesson *everything is not important*; every prospect is not a customer. Be selective with whom you spend your time. Target real customers, real buyers and real business opportunities. If a prospect is dragging his feet, let him know you are ready to move forward when he is, give him your business card or contact information, and move on. If another tells you she can't afford your price, tell her you are looking forward to her call when she can. Should another say he doesn't have the budget this year, tell him thanks for talking with you and that you'll follow up with him next year. When you stop fooling around with prospects who are not real customers, you'll have much more time to find and do business with those that are!

# Green Zone Selling

Three final points to emphasize before we leave The Time Zone:

» **Follow the 25 percent rule of prospecting. Invest at least 25 percent of your time every week looking for new customers and more sales.**

» **Top-producing salespeople are disciplined individuals. As you become more disciplined in how you approach your job and your day, you have more control of your time and get more done.**

» **Success in selling is about spending the right amount of time with the right people. Invest your valuable prospecting time with real customers and real sales opportunities...and watch your business grow!**

For any commissioned salesperson, time truly is money. You only have so much. Use it wisely.

# Part Three
## The Contact Zone

# Making Contacts, Making Friends

Not long ago I listened to a top industry salesman make a presentation at his company's annual meeting sharing what he had learned in his 20-year selling career about success. He'd broken every sales record in the organization and enjoyed #1 status in the sales force as well as the admiration of senior management and his peers. He told the audience his approach to selling was very simple: that it's all about people and how you make them *feel*. The more sincere and straightforward you approach your customers, the more successful you will be. He summed up his speech in one sentence: "Selling is being paid to make friends."

The profession of selling has always been, is today, and hopefully always will be a people business. New products will come and go. Pricing, packaging and promotions will change. Technology will march ever onward. Through all these transitions, the most successful and highest paid salespeople will always be good people...*who are good with people.*

As you enter into The Contact Zone with me, keep this top salesperson's philosophy in mind. Selling isn't about killing the competition, out-maneuvering your customers or deploying manipulative tactics to get someone to say yes. Selling is about helping people. It's about converting prospects into happy customers by showing them how your product or service or system or solution helps them achieve what they are trying to achieve. Selling is simply being paid to make friends.

# Getting Personal

Another powerful practice and lasting lesson I learned about selling came years ago from a superstar named Tony. (I still remember his name because I still remember his lesson.) I was facilitating a series of role-play scenarios in a face-to-face selling skills workshop and I asked the observers—including Tony—to comment on the last salesperson's performance in the role-play. "Stop saying we," Tony told the man. Everyone, including me, was confused with the feedback. But when Tony explained his remark it made perfect sense.

Tony felt strongly that selling is very personal and that people want to do business with people they know, like and feel they can trust. He went on to say that his mission in every sales encounter was to build a positive, *personal* rapport with the people he met.

In doing so, Tony conditioned himself early in his sales career to replace the word "we" with the word "I" in his vocabulary as much as possible. Instead of saying, "We have some good solutions for you," he says: "I have some good solutions for you." Rather than stating: "We want to earn your business," he says: "I want to earn your business." Tony has replaced: "We appreciate your loyalty to our company," with: "I appreciate your loyalty to me." (This is incredibly powerful sales training you are going through at this moment and I want you to wrap your brain around it. In 30 years of selling, very few tips I have discovered have been more simple, profound or useful.)

If you think about this mode of selling, Tony is dead right. Most people don't do business with a company, but with a person. I bank at a very large financial institution with over 50,000 employees. But I know Seth, just Seth. He takes care of me and my banking needs. My financial plan, annuity, life insurance and retirement programs are with a mammoth, worldwide corporation. But I don't know anyone there except Jim. He's my advisor and go-to guy. I get my hair cut at a busy neighborhood salon. Erin is my stylist. I really don't know the 10 or 12 other women there. I go see Erin. And here's the kicker: If Seth, Jim or Erin ever changed companies and went somewhere else, I'd likely follow right behind. My personal relationship with them is more bonding than my loyalty to the company where they work.

Most people do business with people, not companies. That means you should first and foremost establish yourself as the *person* the customer wants to do business with. Practice these lines:

*"What can I do for you next?"*
*"I want to send you some information in the mail."*
*"How does what I offer compare with other offers you have seen?"*
*"How would you rate the service I have given you so far?"*
*"I have the knowledge and experience to do a great job for you."*
*"I want to earn your referrals. Do you know anyone else I can help?"*

Make selling personal. Stop saying "we" and start saying "I" as you present your capabilities and communicate with your customers. People may find it easy to say no to your company, your product, your price or your terms. They will find it much harder to say no to *you*.

# Get in Focus

There are two distinct styles of interactive selling. First, there is the approach that focuses on the salesperson. The second, and far more successful method, is the style that focuses on the customer. Here, for example, is a comment focused on the salesperson:

*"Mr. Jones, I'd like to set up an appointment so I can come out and tell you about the exciting products and services we have to offer."*

And here is the style that is focused on the customer:

> *"Mr. Jones, I'd like to set up an appointment*
> *so I can find out a little more about your needs*
> *and see if what I have can help you."*

Take off your sales shoes for a moment and walk in the customer's shoes. If you were a customer, which style would appeal more? It is unfortunate that many companies, books and sales training courses teach the wrong approach to selling. Their mantra is:

> *Sell, sell, sell!*
> *Control the conversation!*
> *If you don't let the customer talk, he can't say no!*

With this line of attack, selling becomes an adversarial game. It is offense (the salesperson) versus defense (the customer). When your game plan for selling is all about you, it leaves nothing for the customer. And as we know, if the customer detects your advances are all about you and he sees no benefit for himself, he'll say no and walk away, or just hang up.

I'm here to tell you loud and clear that a me-focused, aggressive approach to selling doesn't work. It's crap. If you've been taught to sell that way, end it today. It's self-centered, out of date, and just plain stupid. It is also why so many salespeople's results are not what they should be. They are struggling or failing—not because of what they sell or who they sell for—but because *how* they have been selling is completely wrong.

Get off your agenda and get on the customer's agenda. Tailor your sales approach from the *customer's* point of view, not your own. Notice the following contrasts:

Change: *"Let me tell you about our company."*
To: *"Tell me more about your company."*

Change: *"We've been very successful with this product."*
To: *"Our customers have been very happy with this product."*

Change: *"Do you have any referrals for me?"*
To: *"Who do you know who I can help the way I helped you?"*

The days of badgering and cajoling customers went away with the door-to-door vacuum cleaner salespeople of yesteryear. This is the 21ˢᵗ Century. Your customers are smarter and worldlier than they were years ago. They recognize whether they are sitting in front of a salesperson who cares about them or one who does not. When you show a customer that you are there to help and to serve his or her needs, you connect better, build stronger relationships, and close more sales. It has been said by so many successful salespeople in so many ways:

*"Customers would rather buy than be sold."*

*"Customers don't care how much you know
until they know how much you care."*

*"Help customers get what they want,
and they'll give you what you want."*

While all of these may be just clever little quotes, together they scream out a mammoth message every salesperson needs to hear and heed: *Hey! It's not about you! It's about the customer!*

# Green Zone Selling

You are now in The Contact Zone and exploring successful ways to interact with your customers. Here's a recap of the first three:

» **Selling is being paid to make friends.  If you make friends with your customers, they will buy from you and they'll be your customers forever.**

» **Make selling personal.  Exchange the word "we" with the word "I" as much as possible when speaking with your customers.**

» **Get off of your agenda and get on your customer's agenda.  Talk less about yourself, your company and your products or services. Talk more about them.**

Top salespeople, like top athletes, understand the importance of practicing and honing their skills. Selling is a skill that must be learned and practiced to be mastered.  So let's learn more...

# Making Sales or Making Excuses

It was a small room, a conference room, with about 15 people present. I was to deliver a personal marketing workshop to this group of salespeople right after they held their branch's monthly progress meeting. The room was unnaturally quiet. I knew that the branch had not been doing well and several members of the team were on notice. I was brought in to help.

The sales manager started the meeting with a report on sales production and a few other news items about product changes and systems upgrades from corporate. Then he put down his pad, paused for a moment, took off his glasses and started speaking from the heart. "Guys, I don't have to tell you we're in trouble. Some of you are doing okay, but most are not. Sales are off and our numbers are pretty dismal. I think I know the problem. We're making too many excuses for our lack of results. We say we can't get our production up because of our prices, because of our products, because of our delivery system, because of…well, you fill in the blank." I could tell he had the group's attention. I could also tell from a lot of somber faces that the salespeople knew he was right. He had in effect "called them out." Then the sales manager said something I thought was so incredibly powerful I not only wrote it down but have repeated it in over a hundred seminars and sales presentations since:

> *"You are either making sales or you are making excuses.*
> *Those making sales have few excuses.*
> *And those making excuses have few sales."*

Any salesperson can come up with a hundred excuses for poor sales performance. Among the most common are; a bad economy, too much competition, high pricing, lack of sellable product, a slow time of year, not enough advertising dollars, no brand recognition and inefficient delivery systems. Some salespeople are masters at creating every conceivable excuse for poor performance. For them, it is easier to make excuses than it is to make sales.

I can think of only one reason why successful salespeople do so well: It is because they are making sales. They know they could also come up with all sorts of excuses why they can't sell even more, but they don't. They have no time or desire to sit around and concoct lame excuses. Instead, they are investing their time and energy into prospecting, networking, following up, meeting customers and making sales.

If you are a sales manager, never allow your salespeople to "excuse" themselves from good performance. If you are a salesperson, don't let excuses be the grounds for arguing a case of poor results. If your company truly does not have a quality product or a competitive price or good customer service, get out. Quit today and go to work for another outfit where you can make a good living. If your industry is in such bad shape because of the economic climate and you see no reprieve in the near future, leave. Pack up your skills and experience and talents and go find a better sales career in an industry where you can earn good money and make a difference. Hanging around where you are now and making excuses for your performance problems will never help you or anyone else around you. As a matter of fact, people will just see you as a moaner and complainer and someone who defends their own incompetence with an endless litany of excuses. (Not exactly the image you want to portray, is it?)

Even if you are doing well right now but feel you could do better, never make excuses for why you are not. If you can do something about it, do it. Either take action or don't. If there is a legitimate reason you can't climb to the next level and it is outside of your control, accept your current standing for the time being and don't whine about it. (Remember The Serenity Prayer?)

One more time, just so you never forget:

*"You are either making sales or you are making excuses.*
*If you are making sales you have few excuses.*
*If you are making excuses you have few sales."*

# The Curse of Call Reluctance

We all know where sales come from: Sales come from sales activities like networking, advertising, marketing, and making consistent contact with people and prospects. That being understood, there is one thing that stops most salespeople from making the contacts it takes to generate more sales. This "curse" is the main reason why many folks would never consider a career in selling and it is why so many in the profession perform poorly, quit, or eventually get fired. It's a killer of sales careers. It is called *sales call reluctance.*

At its core, sales call reluctance is a psychological fear of prospecting. Essentially, it is you talking yourself out of making contacts (calling prospects, setting up appointments, asking for referrals, etc.) because of some fear you have fabricated in your mind. This fear manifests itself in many ways. For some salespeople it is...

- A fear of being rejected
- A fear of being a pest or a bother to people
- A fear of being intimidated by a prospect
- A fear of how people might perceive your intentions
- A fear of failure

If sales call reluctance is the killer of sales careers, and your career is suffering, it could be killing yours right now. Or, if your results to this point have been good and you're stuck on a plateau in your sales production, it may be what's holding you back from reaching that next level. Either way, this fear has to be overcome if you are to move forward into the Green Zone.

To beat the curse of sales call reluctance you have to understand what it is and where it comes from. First, it's not real. Sales call reluctance doesn't actually exist in physical form. *It's how you think.* It is a negative notion you manufacture in your head. Second, sales call reluctance feeds itself; the more you dwell on it the stronger it becomes. It's like a cancer that grows and grows. Fear creates more fear until you get to the point where you are so afraid to reach out and make contacts that you choose to sit back and do nothing at all. Yikes!

If you are sometimes stopped cold by sales call reluctance, let's work together right now to see if we can "fix" the way you think. To overcome sales call reluctance you have to change your outlook about making sales contacts from *negative* expectations to *positive* expectations. Consider this: If you think you are going to fail, you won't even try. If you think you'll get rejected, you won't make the contact. See how call reluctance works? When you project your thoughts into a selling situation and anticipate a *negative* result, you won't take action. You'll make fewer calls, initiate fewer contacts, close fewer sales and make less money. A negative outlook creates negative results. (See how what we covered in Part One: The Mind Zone applies here?)

When you project your thoughts into a selling situation and see a potentially *positive* result, you are more likely to move forward. You'll make more calls, more contacts, more sales and more money. Let's contrast this lesson in a few examples:

Negative mindset: *This guy probably already has a company or rep he deals with. I'd be surprised if I got an appointment with him.*
Positive mindset: *This guy fits the profile as someone needing my services. He may be open to talking with me.*

Negative mindset: *I already phoned this woman once and left a message. She's probably not interested or she would have called me back by now.*
Positive mindset: *I need to call this woman back immediately. She seemed interested when we talked the other day. She'll be impressed that I took the initiative to follow up.*

Negative mindset: *I'd be wasting my time sending out these letters. No one is going to respond.*
Positive mindset: *If I get only one sale out of these twenty letters the commission I earn will be well worth the time I've spent.*

See the difference? You must defeat the negative overtones of sales call reluctance with positive mind power; offset negative thinking with positive thinking. Project your thoughts into the sales situation and see a potentially positive outcome, not a negative one. See yourself getting the appointment. See yourself answering phone calls from your marketing efforts. See yourself having intelligent conversations with customers. See your hard work and sales contacts paying off in new clients, new business opportunities and more money.

Does "seeing" a positive result guarantee it will happen? Of course not. But if you see a positive outcome and expect good things to happen as a result of your sales contacts, you are more likely to do them. And when you do them, you have an *infinitely* better chance of finding a new customer or landing another sale than if you don't. And that's the point of this lesson and another bit of age-old sales wisdom:

> *You have a much better chance at landing a sale if you make a contact than if you don't.*

If you've been cursed by sales call reluctance in the past, put it in the past! Liberate yourself from constant negative (red) thinking and switch to a mindset of positive (green) thinking. You will be astonished at the difference it will make in your attitude and your results.

(If you want even more ideas for dealing with call reluctance, the next lesson is a home run!)

# Sales is Like Baseball

In selling, it is common and expected to fail more than you succeed. Not every prospect becomes a customer. Not every customer says yes. Not every big deal goes down the way you thought it would. As a matter of fact, more people will say no to you in your sales career than will say yes. That's the way it works. Sales is like baseball.

Think about a major league baseball player. A good batting average is around .300. For you non-baseball fans, that means he succeeds in reaching base about 30 percent of the time and strikes out, flies out, grounds out or just plain gets called out about 70 percent of the time. He fails at his job seven out of ten times he tries. Does he still get paid? You bet! Bat .300 in major league baseball consistently and you'll earn around five to ten million dollars a year. (What a great job!)

You have to approach selling the same way a ballplayer approaches major league baseball. You must expect to fail in your prospecting efforts as much as 70 to 80 percent of the time. This is a harsh reality of the selling business, but one you need to think about...especially if you have a touch of sales call reluctance.

Suppose you phoned 10 potential prospects and asked for an appointment or a meeting. It's likely seven or eight will say no and maybe two or three will say yes. That's how selling works. You may present your product or service over a hundred times a month to make 20 sales, perhaps less depending on the nature of your industry. Hey; get used to it. That's how selling works.

You probably heard a long time ago that selling is a "numbers" game and here's where that wisdom applies. For example:

Jim is a salesperson. He makes, on average, 2 sales contacts per day. In the course of a month, his efforts add up to about 40 contacts total. If Jim is successful converting 20 percent of his contacts to sales, (batting .200) Jim will close 8 sales a month.

Jan is a salesperson who works alongside Jim. Jan makes, on average, 4 sales contacts per day. In the course of a month, her efforts add up to about 80 contacts total. If Jan is equally skilled as Jim in converting 20 percent of her contacts to sales, Jan will close 16 sales a month.

By making just two more contacts per day, Jan generates eight more sales every month and earns twice the money Jim earns. Jim could double his income, not by becoming a better salesperson, but by following Jan's daily contact numbers and making only two more contacts every day. Not twenty. Not even ten. *Just two.*

To yield twice as many sales, Jan will have to hear "no" a lot more often than Jim. If Jim makes 40 contacts a month and nets 8 sales, he hears some form of "no" or gets turned down 32 times. Jan makes 80 contacts a month, nets 16 sales, but has to hear some form of "no" 64 times. Jan understands how the game of selling is played, she steps up to bat more than Jim, and that's the only reason why she's closing more sales and making twice the money.

I want you to become a better, sharper, more effective sales professional—and the many ideas in this book will help you do that. However, sometimes it really is about *quantity*, not quality. Selling, like baseball, is a game of numbers. You can become the best, most knowledgeable and professional salesperson in your company, your market, even your industry. But if you can't get up to bat and take a lot of swings at opportunities every day, it won't matter one bit how much experience or knowledge you have. You still won't make more sales.

As you increase the number of contacts, calls and customer encounters you initiate every day, you will watch your results and income grow and grow year after year. Here's another simple yet interesting exercise:

1. Calculate how many contacts you are making right now on a monthly basis.
2. Estimate your present "batting average." What percent of your contacts convert into sales?
3. Increase your number of contacts by 20 percent per month.
4. Using the same batting average, calculate how many more sales you could close each month.
5. How does that look to you?

# Green Zone Selling

Here's a 60-second review of the three lessons we just studied:

» **You are either making sales or you are making excuses. If you have been making excuses for your results, stop! Start making sales.**

» **Sales call reluctance is a curse and a killer of careers. Shift your mind away from a fearful, negative way of thinking about making sales contacts to a positive one. You'll take more action and yield more results.**

» **Sales is like baseball. You'll strike out more than you'll score. Go for more "at bats" every day (contacts, appointments, phone calls, etc.) and your sales results will quickly improve.**

Selling is a contact sport. Put yourself in contact with more people more often and you will meet more prospects, uncover more opportunities, land more sales and make more money!

# The "First Five"

Something new called "speed dating" entered the singles scene a few years ago. Although I've never actually participated in the ritual, I saw it demonstrated on a reality TV show once and that makes me an expert on the subject. Here's how it works.

A number of women are seated individually at small tables in a room (often in a restaurant). Each woman wears a number. An equal number of men show up, also wearing numbers. Each man is paired with a woman for exactly five minutes so they can meet each other and talk about whatever they want. A whistle sounds and the men move to the next table. This procedure is repeated until every guy has talked with every girl. If the woman is interested in spending more time with certain men, she writes their numbers on her form. The men do the same with the women they meet. When all is over, the matchmaking service compiles and compares the numbers. If the interest turns out to be mutual, contact information such as phone numbers and email addresses are shared and the connections are made. (Isn't love grand?)

Speed dating is based on a great deal of sociological research that suggests most people develop distinct opinions about another human being within the first five minutes of meeting. We commonly identify with this as a "first impression." First impressions are very powerful things, not just in matters of the heart, but in selling as well.

Your customers will form a first impression of you. How you dress, how you walk, how you wear your hair and how you carry yourself all send signals about the type of person you are...or the person the customer believes you to be. You may be more comfortable with your hands in your pockets, but many people see that as too casual, even threatening—like you are hiding something. You may look like a cool dude in your goatee and longer hair, but does it resonate the right way with the type of customers you serve? Some saleswomen come on very strong with a mile wide smile, a booming voice and an armful of bracelets that jingle like sleigh bells when they shake your hand. Does that sort of first impression work in your line of business to pull prospects toward you...or does it scare them away?

Pay closer attention to the first impressions you are making with your customers, especially within those precious first five minutes. That "first five" can either make or break your chances of a sale, let alone a potential long-lasting client relationship.

Here are some ideas to consider. They may seem like common sense, but many salespeople just don't do them:

- If you have a business breakfast or lunch appointment with a customer, show up on time—maybe even a few minutes early.
- Dress the part of the person you are: a top notch, well-informed and highly-skilled sales professional.
- If you are approaching a customer in your office, a showroom, or on a trade show floor, approach him or her slowly and with your hands to your side.
- Greet people with a standard "Hello" or "Good morning" or "Welcome." Avoid the more casual "What's up?" or "C'mon in!" or as a salesperson said to me the other day in a computer store, "My man! What can I do you for?" Please.
- Look at your customer's face, make solid eye contact, and focus completely on your conversation.
- Avoid quick gestures, wild arm movements, loud hand-clapping and boisterous laughs.
- Beware of getting into people's personal space (less than two feet from their body).
- Smile a genuine smile—like when you are greeting an old friend.

In the coming lessons, I'm going to move you through the sales process from start to finish beginning with the skill of *connecting*. You'll learn how to use that fabulous first five minutes to connect with your customers...and to a lot more sales!

# Connecting

How many new potential prospects do you talk with in the course of a year? I don't expect you to know the exact answer, just take an approximate guess. (It's probably a pretty sizable number.) Now answer another question: What percent of those prospects become customers? Is it 5 percent? Maybe 25 percent? Could it be as high as 50 percent? In sales, this calculation is called "capture rate" and echoes our earlier work comparing sales to baseball batting averages. So, what's your capture rate?

It's my guess you'd like to improve your capture rate. If you can, you'll be able to close more sales while talking to the same number of (or fewer) prospects, thus freeing up even more time to find more opportunities to make more money. There are several ways to do this, as I will show you here in The Contact Zone. As a start, let's go even deeper into that all-important first five minutes and find out.

"Connecting" with customers is the way super-successful salespeople get off to a great start. It's more than just an art; it's a science. Like any science, it can be broken down and analyzed in its elements and studied. Here are the five keys to connecting with customers:

1.  Establish and maintain solid eye contact. Eye contact shows you are focused, attentive and honest. Avoid the tendency to look down too much at your forms and brochures, at the product you are demonstrating, or even out the window at others walking by. And don't you dare attempt to multi-task by looking at your computer screen or your cell phone! Zero in on the customer. Right now, in this moment, that person is your entire world.

2.  Smile. A warm, welcoming smile sends the signal that

you are glad to be there and that you are a nice, happy person to get to know.

3.  Capture the customer's name and use it in conversation. The best way to find out a customer's name is to offer yours first. For example: "Good afternoon, my name is Doug. And you are?" You'll find 99 percent of the time the customer will reply by offering you his or her name, like: "I'm Marcie."

    Now that you know the person's name, use it! Insert the customer's first name into the conversation several times. For example: "How can I help you, Marcie?" and "Marcie, is that what you are looking for?" People love the sound of their own names. Using it will constantly keep you connected throughout the conversation.

4.  Match your pace to that of the customer's. There are a number of books, seminars and teachings out here telling salespeople to "adapt" their style to the customer's style or mentally put people into one of four "boxes" based on what you perceive the customer's persona to be. This is hogwash. When you alter your personality to every customer you meet based on who they are and how they behave, you come across as phony or fake. It's not how you normally talk or act, so why pretend to be someone you are not? (Sales is not acting, it's selling!)

    You can, however, speed up or slow down your *pace* based on the customer's comfort zone. If you are meeting with a customer who speaks and progresses leisurely, slow down a bit. If you are on the phone with someone who is moving a mile a minute, pick up your pace. Work at the tempo that suits your customer. In short: Don't change your style, but do adjust your speed.

5. Move the customer *forward*. Small talk and rapport building are nice, and taking time to get to know a customer will serve you well. But let's face it; neither of you are there strictly for social reasons. Remember that your time is money and your customer has other things to tend to that day. Questions like: "How would you like to get started?" or "What would you like to see?" are all excellent ways to move your customer, the conversation and the potential sales opportunity forward.

# Listen Up!

There was a major study published recently about customer perceptions of salespeople. An independent survey firm met with over 500 individuals and asked them about their experiences with salespeople. As you might imagine, the comments ran the gamut from high praise to total disgust. What was most interesting was the answer to this question: *What is one thing you feel most salespeople could do better?*

Over 90 percent of the respondents said the same thing: listen. Here is a selection of the actual comments these customers made:

> *"All salespeople do is talk. Talk! Talk! Talk!"*
> *"I wish they would shut up once in a while."*
> *"Most of the time you can tell they're not really listening."*
> *"They never let you say anything. They just keep talking."*
> *"Good salespeople know how to keep quiet and let their customers talk."*

Listening has to be one of the easiest things to do. You just have to listen. That's all. You don't have to talk, strategize or present. Just listen. So if listening is so easy, why did 90 percent of those customers surveyed say salespeople don't do it very well?

Perhaps it comes down to how some see their "role" as a salesperson. If you feel that you are responsible to sell, deliver, promote, persuade, convince, pitch and influence, you'll probably talk a lot and not do very much listening. On the other hand, if you see your role as more of a consultant—someone interested in finding out what a customer wants and needs so you can help him or her—you'll just naturally listen more.

Remember that people love to talk about the greatest topic in the world: Themselves! Let them. Encourage them. These tips will help:

- Keep constant eye contact with your customer. Direct eye contact says: "I am interested in you and I'm listening. Talk to me!"

- Ask good questions. Questions put the emphasis on the customer and take it off of you, and that's exactly what you want. (More good stuff on this in a moment.)

- If the sales situation lends itself, take notes. When your customer sees you writing notes on what he or she is saying, they will keep talking. (Try it; it works!)

- Use verbal signals like: "Tell me more," or "What else is important to you?" or "That's interesting!" All of these will promote more dialogue.

- Use non-verbal signals like head nodding or an inquisitive look. People can read your body language better than you realize. Send the message that you *want* them to talk.

- Briefly summarize or paraphrase key points or statements the customer makes. This says that you have listened, and as the survey said, customers would like to see their salespeople listen a whole lot more.

# Green Zone Selling

We're moving deep into the interactive selling skills part of this book now. To summarize the last three lessons:

» **First impressions are not only lasting, they are more important than we realize for attracting new customers. The first five minutes you spend with a prospect sets the stage for your entire interaction. Make your first impression a good one.**

» **Take the time to connect with your customers. A warm smile, solid eye contact, using his or her name in conversation and following a comfortable pace will all serve you well.**

» **Most salespeople talk too much. Be aware of your "talk time" with a customer. Talk less and listen more. You'll make a better impression and learn what people really want.**

Even if you are an experienced sales professional, you still need to keep your selling skills sharp. It makes a difference in the conversations you have and the results you get every day.

# Any Questions?

As we now know, it is a myth to believe that selling is all about talking. One of the biggest mistakes many salespeople make— even veteran salespeople who should know better—is to think that "the pitch" is everything in selling and the more you can keep your lips moving, the better. Few things could be further from the truth. In fact, the best salespeople are not necessarily the best talkers. The best and most successful salespeople are great *listeners* (flashback!) and they became great listeners by learning how to ask great questions. Open your mind to this truth:

*It is the ability to ask the right questions that leads to most sales.*

Whether the customer is considering buying a home, a car, an insurance policy, a cleaning service, a certificate of deposit or a new laptop computer, the salesperson who can ask the right questions to discover the customer's real wants, concerns and needs will most likely both land the sale and secure the customer for future business…and referrals!

In your customer conversations, you want to reach a "balance" of talk time. A balanced conversation means you are talking about 50 percent of the time and the customer is talking about 50 percent of the time. So, in a 10 minute phone conversation, your ears should be working five minutes and your mouth should be moving no more than five minutes. In a one-hour face-to-face meeting, you are allowed to talk 30 minutes throughout the interaction and the customer has 30 minutes. The only way that is going to happen is if you are an attentive listener (as we just covered) and you are proficient in the art of asking really good questions.

Back in Sales Training 101 you presumably learned about the difference between "closed" questions and "open" questions. Closed questions are those that require a one word answer.

These questions typically start with the words: do, are, can, is, will, would and could. Examples:

*"Do you have a moment to talk?"*
*"Are you interested in getting together?"*
*"Can you call me back?"*
*"Is this something important to you?"*
*"Will you be in on Friday?"*
*"Would you please fill out this form?"*
*"Could you find this feature useful?"*

Closed questions are best used when trying to verify specific information, confirm arrangements, or move a customer to action.

Open questions, by contrast, typically require a more detailed response. Often referred to as "reporter questions," open questions are purposely designed to stimulate meaningful thought, create a conversation and gather valuable information you can use to help a customer make the right decision. These are commonly called "what" questions. Some examples:

*"What are you looking for today?"*
*"What are your concerns about this product?"*
*"What should I know about your business?"*
*"What would you like to learn about my services?"*
*"What are three things I could be doing for you right now?"*
*"What do you like about my proposal?"*
*"What questions can I answer for you today?"*
*"What are your next steps?"*

The right questions get you the right information. They show your customers you are focused on their situation and their needs. Open questions also help you reach that 50/50 talk-time balance you want. Above all, great questions move the sales process forward and allow you to present the right solutions. And while we are on the subject of questions…

# Answer One with Another

Here's a short but useful selling skill to remember: Answer a question with a question. This lesson is best illustrated with examples, so let's start there:

Customer: *"Does this come in blue?"*
Salesperson: *"I'll have to check to see if we have it in blue. Is blue the only color you would consider?"*

Customer: *"Why does it weigh so much?"*
Salesperson: *"It's a very solid and well-made product. Are you going to travel with it a lot?"*

Customer: *"Why are you guys priced higher than everybody else?"*
Salesperson: *"What other prices are you seeing out there?"*

See how this works? The right questions, carefully placed, will expand the conversation with the customer and help you find out their true concerns. Often times, what customers ask about on the surface are not their real reservations. In other instances, replying to a question with a question helps you to leave other options open. Let's look at more examples:

Customer: *"Why does it take so long to ship?"*
Salesperson: *"When is the date you must absolutely have it?"*

Customer: *"How much experience do you have with this product?"*
Salesperson: *"I've sold this successfully for three years now. What specifically are you concerned about?"*

Customer: *"Why are these fees so high?"*
Salesperson: *"Each fee covers different costs. Can I go over them with you right now?"*

Are you getting the hang of it? Sometimes in my selling skills seminars I have participants write down common questions they receive from their customers. Then, we construct response questions for each one. Not only is this a fun exercise, it is a great conditioning drill for how to address questions you frequently get from your customers. (You might want to do this now yourself. Take out a sheet of paper, make a list of five or six recurrent questions you get from your customers and develop a response question—not an answer—for each one.)

If selling is a skill—which it is—it must be practiced and polished to be perfected.

# Presenting Solutions

Few things are more rewarding to a sales professional than the ability to pull off a really great sales presentation. Being able to package and present your product or service solution to a customer and have him or her say: "Yes! That's what I want!" is what living in the Green Zone of selling is all about.

To get to this stage, other things need to happen first. You need to connect well with your customer, establish a positive first impression, ask the right questions and listen to the answers (as we just covered). If you've done a good job of that, the presentation part comes easy. If you skipped all of that, it will be like throwing darts at a dartboard while blindfolded; you'll just keep missing the mark.

I could write an entire book solely on the subject of presenting solutions. (As a matter of fact, I have several excellent books on my bookshelf from authors who have done just that.) But for now, since we are working to develop your entire sales approach in four different zones, I'll stick to some sound fundamentals of great sales presentations. There are 10 I'll cover, so take your time and study them carefully:

1. **Keep it short and simple.** Attention spans are not what they used to be. When TV first started regular broadcasting in the 1950s, most commercials were two minutes long. Today, the average television commercial is 20 seconds. When it comes time to present your solution to a customer, keep close watch on the clock. Most great solutions presentations are one to two minutes in length. (Again, this depends a great deal on the complexity of your product or service. A real estate agent can't show a house in one minute and someone who sells million-dollar X-ray machines to hospitals may need to take a bit longer. However, for most salespeople, their presentations could stand to be a lot shorter.) Trim it up, present the highlights, keep it to one or two minutes, and then let the customer ask questions about the rest.

2. **Tie your suggestions and solutions directly to the customer's needs.** Every solutions presentation is different because what every customer wants and needs is different. As you talk about your product or service, reflect back on what the customer told you. For example: "Mike, you said that volatility concerns you. Here's how this investment program helps…" or "Karen, one of the things you said a while ago was you wanted to keep your costs down. Let me show you how I can do just that…" The more your customers see how the solution you are presenting directly meets *their* specific needs, the more they will listen to your ideas.

3. **Avoid industry jargon.** Check these out: CSP, OJT, Idea Mapping. You probably have no idea what any of that means, yet those are common terms in the professional speaking and training business I work in every day. You too have a language that is foreign to me…and your customers. Your company, industry and products are filled

with acronyms and expressions nobody outside your world understands. When making a presentation to a customer, stay away from them; they won't impress, only confuse. Confused customers have a harder time saying yes.

4. Present with features, sell with benefits. (My apologies if you are an experienced sales professional and find this too basic, but this bit of simple sales training should never be forgotten and always be practiced.) *Features* talk about what a product is, has or does. *Benefits* translate those features into what they mean to the customer. For example:

Salesperson: *"The car comes standard with anti-lock breaks and eight air bags. Since you said your teenage daughter will also be driving this car, you can feel good that she's in a very safe vehicle."*

Salesperson: *"The mortgage rate on this product is fixed for thirty years. Your monthly principle and interest mortgage payment will never increase. I heard you mention you wanted something safe with no surprises and this would fill those needs."*

Salesperson: *"The annuity provides you with a regular and predictable stream of income in your retirement years. You talked about that being what you wanted most of all."*

Salesperson: *"This printer uses about half the ink of most other brands. You said your last printer ate ink and cost you a fortune. You won't have that added expense with this one."*

Make sure you are adding strong benefits to your product or service features in every solutions presentation. Customers love features, but they always buy benefits.

5. Use visuals to demonstrate. If you are selling a tangible product (a house, a car, a dining room set, a refrigerator, etc.) refer to the product often. Let the customer "experience" the product by seeing it, touching it, smelling it, tasting it, whatever. If you sell an intangible product or service (life insurance, a mortgage loan, investments, consulting services, etc.) you have to learn how to bring your solutions to life. Many successful salespeople do this with presentation packets, brochures, videos, testimonial letters, examples and stories. The more "real" you can make your product or service, the better your customers can envision themselves owning it.

6. Slow down. Many salespeople talk too quickly to hold people's attention. Often times this is out of excitement, or nervousness, or both. The faster you talk, the harder it is for a customer to listen. At this stage of the sales process, the customer is hearing what you have to say, making mental notes, trying to follow along, forming an opinion of what you are presenting and deciding if it is right for him. That's a lot going on all at once. Don't lose him by talking too fast.

7. Take a breath now and then. Don't use run-on sentences. Stop from time to time (three to five seconds) not just to gather your thoughts but to allow the customer to digest what you have said. (Imagine pumping gas into your car at a rate faster than it can hold. The gas just runs out all over the place!) Well-placed pauses invite positive comments, possible concerns and pertinent questions to enter into the presentation—and that's exactly what you want. The more engaged the customer is in your solution, the better chance he will be interested in buying it.

8. Don't over-sell. When you tell a customer your solution is

"perfect" or flawless, he'll immediately become skeptical. Present an honest overview of what your product or service has and does not have, and what it can and cannot do. If you are honest here, the customer will believe you are honest in everything else you say. For example:

Salesperson: *"This house is in a great location and neighborhood. It's not within close walking distance to the school like you wanted, but it is definitely worth considering."*

Salesperson: *"Our pest control service handles most kinds of yard bugs. You'll still see a few grub worms from time to time, but I'll be able to take care of most of your problems and really improve the looks of your lawn."*

9.  **Present from point to point.** I've listened to many salespeople hop, skip and jump all over the place when talking about a product or service they are selling. Your customer's brain can't take that. Present feature A and add the benefit to the customer. Then present feature B, add the benefit and so on. Don't jump from point A to B to point C and back to A and then to C and return over to B. Move in a straight line. Follow a linear format, similar to giving someone driving directions for how to get from one place to another. Make your presentation make sense.

10. **Portray a feeling of confidence.** If the customer can see that you feel good about the solution you are presenting, he will feel good about it too. Be definitive in your language and sure in your speech. "So, um, it looks like maybe, uh, we can help you," sounds awful. "Based on what you are looking for, this is certainly a solution to consider," sounds great.

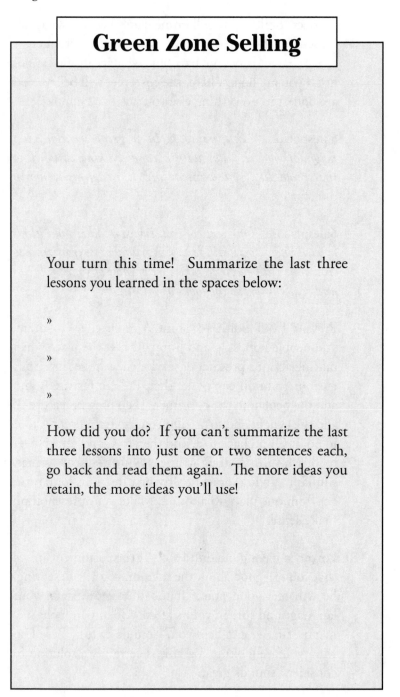

# Green Zone Selling

Your turn this time!  Summarize the last three lessons you learned in the spaces below:

» 

» 

» 

How did you do?  If you can't summarize the last three lessons into just one or two sentences each, go back and read them again.  The more ideas you retain, the more ideas you'll use!

# Sales Speak

There is an old adage: "It's not what you say, but how you say it." One of the attributes I have noticed among highly-successful salespeople is their ability to move a customer to action. This is done primarily through a technique I call "sales speak."

Sales speak is a different way of talking to people. It requires you to be a little less passive and markedly more assertive. It's not about being pushy or aggressive with people, nor is it manipulating a customer to make a decision that he or she is uncomfortable with. Sales speak is shifting from a *reactive* sales approach to a more *proactive* one by altering your choice of words in customer conversations. As before, this skill is best illustrated in examples, so let's see a few:

> Reactive: *"When do you want to meet?"*
> Proactive: *"Let's set up a time to meet this week. What day works best for you?"*
>
> Reactive: *"Just send me that information when you can."*
> Proactive: *"To get this done quickly, I'm going to need that information from you by Friday. Can you do that?"*
>
> Reactive: *"Would you like to think about this some more?"*
> Proactive: *"If this is what you are looking for, and the price is right, I suggest we go through the specifics."*
>
> Reactive: *"Call me back when you can."*
> Proactive: *"I'm in the office today. My number is 681-8004. Please call me back before five o'clock."*

Perhaps this is a skill you have already mastered. If so, it is likely that your sales speak has served you well. On the other hand, if this concept is foreign to you, now would be a good time to explore its uses. Again—at the risk of being redundant—I am not advocating that you are discourteous to people or that you would attempt to maneuver them into buying something they neither want nor need. Rather, I am teaching you a selling skill that is practiced by just about every top salesperson I have ever met. They are not passive in their approach (reactive selling) they are asserting and intentional in providing suggestions and solutions to their customers and then asking for some form of action (proactive selling). That's another reason why they are so successful.

Top producers take control of their opportunities, and to do that, they have to take control of the sales process and their customer conversations. They speak in a more assumptive manner than do other salespeople. They don't wait for things to happen—they make things happen.

The best way to learn sales speak is to eavesdrop on a top producer. Pay attention to how he or she talks to a prospect on the telephone, in a meeting, or when delivering a client presentation. It's very deliberate, very directing, and very much in control. Go to school on this lesson, learn it well, and start to listen carefully to how you speak to people. If selling is mostly about words then what you say and how you say it can mean the difference between a customer who responds to you with a "Let me think about it," and one who says: "Okay, sounds great!"

## Asking for Action

In the iconic sales movie *Glengarry Glen Ross*, the company's regional manager (played by Alec Baldwin) proclaims to his team of high-pressure real estate salesman in a profanity-peppered sales meeting rant: "A-B-C: Always Be Closing!" While this makes for entertaining cinema, it falls flat in the real world. Salespeople who are always closing will push away far more potential prospects than they will keep. Think about it this way; if you were being pressured and badgered by a forceful salesperson, what would you do? You'd walk away or hang up. That's what your prospects are also going to do if you are foolish enough to follow such an abrasive approach with them.

There is a natural process customers go through when they are making a buying decision, and therefore, a natural process sales professionals must adhere to when selling. Although this process can be adapted to various sales situations and buying cycles, 90 percent of the time it can be condensed down to five simple steps:

1. Meet or talk with a prospect and establish a rapport.
2. Discover his or her wants and needs.
3. Present a great solution.
4. Respond to any questions or concerns.
5. Ask for action.

While this sequence may seem blatantly obvious, many salespeople (especially the high-pressure types) don't follow it. They make the mistake of shifting step five up the order by asking for decisions and actions far too soon. In their zeal to close a sale and earn a commission, they completely skip rapport building or don't ask good questions or ignore a customer's objections or concerns. They just keep closing. The result? A customer who says goodbye and goes away.

Let's put a professional spin on the A-B-C approach to asking for action—one that will work far better than the "Always Be Closing" version portrayed in the movie and one that will land you considerably more customers and closed sales.

A: *Ask* for what you want in a statement form.
B: Sell the key *benefits* of taking action.
C: *Confirm* agreement with a question.

Let's see if you can spot the A-B-C skill in the following examples:

*"Mr. Taylor, I'd like to move ahead with your financial plan. I am confident that working together we can build a package that's going to get you that return you want from your investments. Shall we get started today?"*

*"Patty, I'd like to set up an appointment with you for next week. If you and I could spend an hour together, I will show you how this program works for your situation. Can you meet on Monday?"*

*"Ken, I see the next step as a presentation to your executive committee. If you can get me just fifteen minutes in front of them, I can walk them through all the specs and financial details, answer their questions and give them all the information to make the right decision. Can you help set that up?"*

*"Tom, I'd like to suggest you make an offer on this house. It meets most all of your needs, it's priced well within your budget, and if we start the process today, it's likely you could be living here by the end of next month. Would you like to sit down and write up the offer?"*

See the power of this skill? These requests work better not just because they conform to the A-B-C method, but because they incorporate several of the other ideas we covered earlier:

- Use the customer's name in conversation.
- Make selling personal; use "I" versus "we."
- Apply sales speak. Be direct and deliberate in your words.
- Sell with benefits important to the customer.
- Focus on the customer. It's all about helping them and making friends!

# Following Up

I'm going to break with tradition on this practice, so be warned that what I am about to suggest may fly in the face of previous sales training and teachings you've experienced.

I've always been led to believe that continual follow up on potential prospects was critical to success in selling. "Keep calling until they buy or die!" a sales manager once told me. "Follow up with a prospect at least ten times before you give up!" said another. While this sounds like it should be good advice, in the real world it rarely pays off. Let me present my case.

Not everyone out there wants or needs what you are selling. As we already learned, you may have to make a lot of contacts to land a few prospects. Of those prospects who might be somewhat interested in what you offer, not every customer will move forward, can afford to move forward, or will choose you or your product or your company to fill their needs. (Remember, you aren't the only game in town. You have lots of competitors out there selling the same thing you do.) Any salesperson can expect to capture only a percentage of their prospects and convert only a percentage of those to actual sales. That's just the way it works. (Like baseball.)

You can waste an *absurd* amount of time following up on leads and prospects who will never buy from you. (I often refer to this scenario as knocking on a door that will never open because essentially there's no one home!) I have witnessed many salespeople quit the business out of frustration because they pour too much energy into following up on dead-end opportunities that aren't opportunities at all. They think that if they just keep calling and following up, the prospect will eventually wear down and buy. The opposite is typically true; the person will just get annoyed, avoid your advances, and *never* buy from you because you came across as too desperate or ticked him or her off so badly with your aggressiveness. (I once actually heard a customer scream at a salesperson: "What part of NO do you not understand?")

Years ago, I began using the "three strikes and you're out" process of follow up. (Yes I know, another baseball analogy. But I promise this is the last one.) If I talk with a prospect who seems interested in my services, I'll typically follow up immediately with a letter or packet of information in the mail. If I don't hear back within five to ten days, I'll follow up with a nice email message. If I get no response from either, I'll make a phone call five to ten days later that goes something like this:

> *"Ron, this is Doug Smith following up as I always do. I mailed you some information that you asked for a few weeks ago and I sent you an email after that. I haven't heard back from you. If you are not interested, that's fine. But if you are interested in talking, I'd enjoy a conversation with you very soon. You can reach me at 877-430-2329. I have some conference calls and appointments, but I am in the office the rest of this week. I'll leave it up to you. Call me if I can help."*

The ball is now in the prospect's glove. I have made three clear, outward attempts to contact him. If he is truly a prospect—interested, qualified and capable of affording my services—he'll call me back. If he does not respond after three attempts to contact him in the span of 15 to 20 days, any further efforts on my part have proven to be a complete waste of my time.

I know what you are thinking: "Why not keep trying? What have you got to lose?" What I've got to lose is precious time, and like you, I know the hourly value of my time and that my time is worth a lot of money. I'd rather invest that time finding and contacting other people who might be real prospects and ready-buyers. Since adopting this "three strikes and you're out" policy, I am less frustrated, more productive, and I have more time to go after authentic business opportunities.

As in other ideas I have presented in The Contact Zone of

this book, consider how it applies to your business and sales model. Maybe for you this won't work like it works for me and many other sales professionals. Just don't fool yourself into thinking you've got a prospect when you don't. People who choose to ignore your follow up contacts not once, not twice, but three times are not interested in talking to you or are not interested in buying what you are selling. Move on...and move *forward.*

# Green Zone Selling

We just covered three major skills practiced by top performers:

» **Sales speak is taking control of your customer conversations by shifting from a more passive form of selling to a more proactive form of selling. Take control, make suggestions and offer action steps. That's what the best in the business do!**

» **If you want action, you have to ask for it. Use the A-B-C method: Ask for what you want in a clear statement, sell the benefits of acting, and confirm the customer's interest or agreement with a question.**

» **Following up is important to converting prospects into customers. But don't keep following up on people who are clearly not qualified or not interested! Use the "three strikes and you're out" rule. Make three good attempts, and if the prospect does not respond, move on to the next opportunity. There are plenty more prospects out there!**

# Part Four

## The Future Zone

# Moving Up to the "Next Level"

Salespeople, companies and professional speakers like to use the phrase "next level" a lot. (I believe I've applied it several times so far in this book.) "I need to get my income to the next level," one salesperson says. "We want to take our results to the next level!" barks the CEO. "It's time to raise your business to the next level!" challenges the motivational speaker. But what is the next level? It seems to me that you can't reach a destination until you define it. So here is the definition we will use:

*The next level is a 50 percent improvement*
*over your current results.*

The next level is not about marginal gains or closing one more sale. The next level is a *significant* leap. If you are now earning $100,000 a year, the next level of success for you is $150,000. If you are selling eight units a month, your next level is twelve units a month. If a company's sales volume last year was $200 million, the next level they should shoot for is $300 million.

Clearly, attaining a 50 percent gain is no easy matter for most salespeople and sales organizations; it will take time, effort and discipline to achieve. What should be emphasized is this:

*You cannot take your business to the next major*
*level by making minor adjustments.*

Making one more sales call a day won't do it; neither will a couple of extra letters or phone calls. Incremental additions will create incremental results. We're talking about at least a

50 percent improvement here. Big improvements are the by-product of big moves and/or big changes.

Cathy is a case in point. Cathy is a salesperson I coached not long ago who came to me with an urgent need to improve her results and her income. (As a matter of fact, Cathy was dangerously close to getting fired for poor performance. It would literally take a 50 percent improvement in her performance just for her to keep her job. It helped that she was motivated!)

Working together, Cathy and I made radical changes to her routine. It started with coming to work 30 minutes earlier every day. (That added two and a half hours to her weekly work schedule.) She was to allocate a minimum of two hours a day, every day, for prospecting and customer contact activities; no excuses. As per our plan, Cathy was required to attend at least one out-of-office function each week (group breakfast, luncheon, networking meeting, industry event) and make a minimum of ten outbound prospecting phone calls and five face-to-face sales calls every week. We pulled her away from paling around with other marginal producers and pushed her toward spending more time associating with those that were being successful in her branch office. We began implementing a new database marketing campaign. Cathy and I closely analyzed her prospect list and client base to identify *real* opportunities and *real* customers, at the same time abandoning those that were Low Yield, time consuming and high maintenance. As Cathy put it to me: "You are rocking my boat!" Indeed I was. It needed rocked.

As a result of Cathy's dedication and discipline to our plan, she not only saved her job but became a solid contributor to her sales team within just six months. Cathy achieved a more than 100 percent improvement in her sales and took her income to the "next level." But to accomplish that feat, it took considerable changes in what she was doing and how she was doing it. Big improvements and big additions will always require big changes, but they will lead you to equally big results. Cathy is proof of that.

Look at where you are now in terms of your sales results and income. Calculate what a 50 percent jump would be. Do you like it? Does that number excite you? Great! That's your "next level" of success and your Future Zone. Now put into action a plan of activities and improvements that will take you there. Just remember that incremental changes will only lead to incremental results. Big moves equal big results. That's what getting to the next level is all about. And if you are an experienced salesperson doing okay right now, the biggest challenge you may face in getting to that next level is your willingness to…

# Push Past Complacency

As you journey through your career in selling, it's possible you could get "complacent" with where you are in your results. You may get to the point where business is good, your income is sufficient and your contribution to your company is positive. When that happens, it's all too easy to pull back on your selling and prospecting efforts because now customers are calling you and orders come in almost routinely. This is a time to sit back, relax a bit, and enjoy the benefits of years of hard work. Or is it?

It is this fabulously flawed strategy that wiped out thousands of sales professionals during the recent Great Recession. Business that just came in the door and over the phone for so long evaporated in a few short months. When customers tightened their belts and prospects stopped calling, many salespeople were left stunned and paralyzed. It was especially difficult for the seasoned veterans to cope with this crisis. They had done so well for so long and got used to earning good money. But they had grown complacent in their careers. When the fallout hit they had no idea what to do. They hadn't really marketed themselves in years. Their selling skills had gone soft. Many saw their incomes drop, others left their jobs, and hundreds were let go. As someone who works closely with salespeople every day, it was a painful sight to see.

In any commissioned sales job, you can *never* allow yourself to grow complacent. As soon as you stop moving forward, you start falling backwards. While you may be content with your sales results and your income right now, remember that the world is still marching on, customer expectations are increasing and things are getting more expensive every day. (Remember $1.75 a gallon gas, $29 hotel rooms and taking a family of four out to a nice dinner for $40? Long gone, my friend!)

It's possible that making the major changes necessary to reach a next level of 50 percent more sales and more income may not be on your radar screen right now, but neither should you be sitting back and resting on your laurels. New York Knicks basketball great Dave Debusschere once said: *"While you are relaxing, your opponent is practicing. And when you meet to compete, he's going to win."* Your competitors are getting smarter and better. Customers are getting more informed and more demanding. Your company is raising the bar. The Internet is circumventing your sales and stealing customers and opportunities before you even find them. And selling anything in the next ten years certainly isn't going to get any easier.

Green Zone salespeople are always in motion, always moving forward. They never get complacent in their careers or content with their results. They understand that the action they take today creates the tomorrow they live in.

# What's Your Number?

If I asked you a direct question would you give me an honest answer? Good. Then let me ask you this:

*On a scale of 1 to 10, how good are you at what you do?*

For this assessment, 1 is the lowest score possible. A score of 1 says you are a complete idiot at selling and have absolutely no idea what you are doing. A score of 10 means you are at the pinnacle of your game, a master of your profession, and should be writing a book on selling instead of reading one. The range from bottom to top is 1 up through 10. Give yourself a number...right now.

Got it? Good. Next, write down the names of the other people in your organization you interact with on a regular basis. This list may include your peers, your support team, other salespeople you work around and even your boss and his or her boss. Do that now.

Finally, next to each name place a number score, using the same scale of 1 to 10, showing your opinion of how good they are at what they do. Are they a 1, a 5, a 9? Give each a number. (Be totally honest; they'll never find out you did this!)

Here's the lesson of this exercise:

> *You can't get any better around people*
> *who are no better than you.*

Let's say you rated yourself a truthful 7 at what you do. Everyone you ranked below a 7 cannot help you succeed beyond your current situation. As a matter of fact, as we mentioned earlier, they will likely only hold you back. If your best friend at work is a 5 and the two other salespeople you pal around with are 4s and your boss is a 6, none of these people can teach you a darned thing. (Think about it; there's not much a fifth grader can learn from a third grader that she doesn't already know.)

You can only learn, grow and improve from people smarter and better than you. Country music star Vince Gill is quoted as saying: *"Don't ever be the best musician in the band. You'll never learn anything because you are better than everyone else."* Legendary football quarterback Joe Theismann offers this advice: *"If you really want to get better and smarter than you are, surround yourself with people better and smarter than you are."*

Many salespeople make the mistake of associating with

other people at their same level (or lower levels) of effectiveness. The 6s hang out with the 6s. The 5s feel at ease in the company of other 5s…or lower. This is a bad move. You may be more comfortable and less intimidated among these people, but is that why you are in sales? Is it your goal to come to work every day so you can feel "comfortable?" No! You got into sales for the challenge, the risk, the upside opportunity to earn good money and to achieve success in your life. If that's true (and I know it is) it is *essential* that you expose yourself to people (peers, managers, coaches, trainers, etc.) who are better and smarter than you—people who can help you reach your goals.

People better and smarter than you can show you how to become a better and smarter salesperson. A really great manager can teach you new techniques, approaches, and mentor you to higher performance. A strong support team will free you up to have more time to find and close more sales. Working around great salespeople will inspire you to become equally great. The adverse is equally true: an incompetent sales support team, a lousy manager and poor-producing peers will only bind you from behind. (Remember the old saying: "You can't soar with the eagles if you flock with the turkeys!")

If you are serious about getting in and staying in the Green Zone of success all throughout your sales career, seek out the wisdom and counsel of others smarter, better and more successful than you. Associate with top producers. Have coffee or take lunch with salespeople who have more experience and information than you have. Form an idea-sharing breakfast club with bright people in your company or your industry. Join a local networking group or high-level think tank of well-read and intelligent people. Attend first-class sales seminars and learning events. Hire a personal business coach as a mentor. Work for a manager whose track record of success impresses and perhaps even intimidates you a little.

When you surround yourself with people who are exceptional, you will learn how to become exceptional too.

# Green Zone Selling

We are now in Part Four of *Green Zone Selling*, and concentrating on building your business platform for a successful, rewarding future. To review the first three lessons of The Future Zone:

» **The "next level" is a 50 percent improvement over where you are now. Small changes won't take you there. You'll need to take big steps if you are serious about big results.**

» **Don't fall victim to complacency! Always keep your skills fresh, your customers close to you, and your sales activities in motion.**

» **You can't get better alongside people no better than you. Expose yourself to people who are smarter, more skilled, and more talented than you are.**

Question: What are you willing to do today to get you to where you want to be tomorrow?

# Run Your Business from a Plan

The most successful salespeople work for themselves. They might have some company's logo on their business card or be employed by a national firm, but in their minds they work for themselves.

It is this sense of ownership and accountability that guides the best salespeople in every industry. Their attitude is: "It is not up to my company to make me successful, it's up to me!" They set their own goals, create their own plans and manage their own schedules. They take responsibility to learn, read, study and improve their skills. They don't need to be motivated. They motivate themselves.

It sounds really great to be your own boss, but some heavy baggage comes with that bonus. You have to view your job and career as *your* business, and you truly have to run it like you own it. To do that effectively, you need a plan.

I've seen dozens of different types of business plan templates out there. If you have one you like and use, stay with it. If you don't, let me suggest one. My business plan format has five sections: Goals, Targets, Activities, Improvements, and Rewards. You can build this plan in less than two hours and use it all year. Here's how it works:

1. Start with the end in mind and establish your annual goals. These could be income goals, sales volume goals, unit goals, whatever applies to your line of work. Use specific numbers and be clear on what you are working to achieve. Then, break down those annual goals into monthly goals, weekly goals, maybe even daily goals. For example:

*Goal is 120 sales a year.*
*120 sales a year ÷ 12 months = 10 sales a month.*
*10 sales ÷ 4 weeks a month = 2.5 sales (2-3 sales) per week.*

Next, calculate the average number of prospects and contacts you need based on the capture and conversion rates you have experienced. For example, if you know that about one in five contacts you make or receive yields an interested prospect (a 20 percent capture rate) and that approximately one in four prospects actually follows through to a sale (a 25 percent conversion rate) you can get a picture of how many people you need to talk with to reach your overall goals. Continuing with the previous example:

*2.5 sales per week divided by .25 =*
*10 prospects per week.*
*10 prospects divided by .20 =*
*50 contacts per week.*
*50 contacts a week divided by 5 days =*
*10 contacts per day.*

This salesperson now has a clear idea of the numbers and activities it will take to reach his goals. If he consistently makes ten contacts per day, based on his historical capture and conversion rates, he will likely reach his goal of 2.5 sales a week and 120 sales a year. (Step one will require a calculator and take you all of ten minutes to complete.)

2.  Next, list the key targets of business that will drive those numbers you created. This list might include walk-in or phone-in traffic, contacting past customers, working with strategic business partners, prospecting among friends and family, advertising, and other sources relevant to your industry and company selling model. Who will you target for business? Make a list. (This will take about five minutes.)

3.  Now comes the most robust part of your plan; your sales activities. Think about the most effective sales, marketing, networking and prospecting activities that will generate the most leads and sales opportunities. This might include phone calls, face-to-face visits, group presentations, direct mail marketing, community networking and more. These are called "campaigns." Each key target of business (from step two) needs a sales campaign of specific activities.

    Once your activities are listed for each target, choose the frequency of how often you plan to perform that activity—daily, weekly, monthly, quarterly, semi-annually, annually—and list that next to each activity. (Allow at least 45 minutes for this part of the business plan…and take your time.) Here is an example of a completed sales campaign for one source:

    | *Source: Past Customers* | *Frequency* |
    |---|---|
    | *Letters* | *Monthly* |
    | *Company newsletter* | *Quarterly* |
    | *Holiday cards* | *Annually* |

4.  Under the heading of "Improvements" you should list the changes, updates and enhancements you need to make that will help you execute your plan and achieve your goals. There might be new products or services you need to learn. Perhaps an upgrade of your contact management system is in order. Maybe you need to change your office organization system or update your sales presentation kits. Improvements made every year will help your business run better and smoother every year. (Expect to spend five to ten minutes here.) For example:

*Improvements*
*Completely redesign my web site*
*Work on my phone skills; use scripts more often*
*Spend less time on the computer, more on making contacts*
*Read more industry publications to stay current on trends*

5. Finally, your rewards. If you work hard all year and achieve your goals, how will you celebrate your success? What perks should you attach to your goals to motivate you to stay on your plan? How about a new car? What about a special vacation with a loved one? New kitchen appliances? A Harley-Davidson motorcycle? Rewards for hard work have been a part of our lives since we were little children. They should be a part of your business plan too. (Although this takes only a couple of minutes and some people are weird about including this step, I strongly recommend it. Tying gifts to goals is a great motivator!) For example:

*If I achieve my goal of 120 sales this year:*
*I'll put away $5,000 in my daughter's college fund.*
*We can install new carpet in the family room.*
*We'll be able to afford a winter ski vacation over New Years!*

Every successful business is run from a plan. Yours should be no exception. If you have a business plan already, good for you! Pull it out and follow it. If you don't have a plan for your business, then you don't have a business—you just have a job.

# Act Like an Entrepreneur

When you hear the word "entrepreneur" you typically think of someone who is self-employed, a risk-taker or a person who runs their own business. Our modern interpretation of this

111

term is actually flawed. The word was first coined by French economist J.B. Say around 1800 and refers to: "Someone who shifts resources out of activities and areas of lower yield into activities and areas of higher yield." So, an entrepreneur is not just a self-made millionaire or a man who owns his own pizza shop or a woman who invents things. An entrepreneur is *anyone* who is capable of shifting his or her resources from activities and areas that are least productive and low payoff to activities and areas of higher productivity with bigger payoffs.

A critical component of your future success in selling is thinking and acting more like an entrepreneur. Most salespeople, as a rule, manage their own time and set their own agenda. Compared to a salaried employee at a coffee shop or a book store or a fast food restaurant, commissioned salespeople (like you) are freer to choose where to focus their time, activities and energy. By shifting your time to high yield activities you become increasingly more productive, locate more new sales opportunities, and inevitably make a lot more money.

I have held positions both as an entrepreneur and a salaried employee and I have experienced the difference first hand. As a Senior Vice President and Director of Sales Training and Marketing for a very large financial institution, my mission (according to the job description) was to lead a team of 12 people in delivering top quality sales training programs and resources to more than 1,000 field salespeople. In fact, in the four years I held that position, I and my team actually spent very little time delivering top quality sales training programs to the field. Most of our time, attention and energy were monopolized by meetings, budgets, forecasts, and all varieties of reports and conference calls. Added to that was the requisite paperwork, HR issues, performance reviews, department relocations, and about a trillion other tasks the company and my boss had us doing—most of which had little or nothing to do with our mission of delivering top quality sales training to the field. We directed the majority of our resources and efforts to activities of very low yield. According to the definition, none of us were *entrepreneurs*.

Now that I am an independent business owner and running my own company, I have evolved into a true entrepreneur in every sense of the word. I see things quite differently. I am consciously aware, all day long, of what I am doing with my time and energy to ensure it is directed toward activities that have the highest yield. I have little time (or patience) to spend on menial matters and busy work. Like you, I am a salesperson. I don't earn a salary. I make money when I speak and write and deliver my services to my customers. All else is low yield. Everything else I could possibly do with my time detracts from the highest and best use of my resources: writing, speaking and talking to people.

All the way back in Part One, we talked about the Pareto Principle and the 80/20 Rule of unequal distribution. The Pareto Principle, as applied here to productivity and yield, suggests that 80 percent of your results arise from 20 percent of your efforts and activities. (It's not that 80 percent of what you do is meaningless or a waste of time; it's just that 80 percent of your activities do not contribute directly to your key goals such as meeting more prospects and making more sales and money.) Entrepreneurs understand this. They know that to generate the highest yield (sales and income) you must concentrate more of your time, effort and energy into activities that produce the highest yield. In a nutshell: Identify and multiply.

Okay, let's apply this. Take out a piece of paper (yes, another exercise) and make a list of the specific activities you perform that create tangible results by answering these three simple questions:

- What are the best ways to make the phone ring?
- What are the ideal methods for meeting new prospects?
- What else works to create new leads, customers and referral opportunities?

Chances are you'll end up with a short list—maybe three, five or ten things—and that's perfect. To keep your sales career in high gear, or as an entrepreneur would say: "to enhance your output," you have to invest *more* time doing these things *more* often. Think like an entrepreneur! Whether you are truly self-employed or you sell for a multi-million-dollar corporation, you are in fact an entrepreneur. Your results and your income are shaped by you and your ability to shift your resources and activities into areas of higher yield. The day you fully realize this fact, your world and your future will never be the same.

# Strike a Balance

Achieving a higher level of success in selling can be exhilarating. It can also be addicting. As you start to experience more of everything—more sales, more recognition, more money—it could become all too easy to find yourself "enslaved" by your career. I have seen salespeople destroy their marriages, alienate their families and ignore their health all in the quest for success. Clearly, there is some penalty to pay for being in the top 20 percent of your company or industry and working hard to earn a sizable income. It won't come without sacrifice. Are you willing to pay the price? Most importantly, do you know how to strike a good balance between work and life? Never forget that your mission is not to live to work; it's the other way around.

Here's some coaching I'd like to offer on this subject. To avoid the chance of reaching career burnout or becoming a workaholic:

- Manage your work-time well. Any talented, full-time salesperson should invest 40 to 50 hours working each week. In some cases, you may want or need to put in extra time to take advantage of immediate sales opportunities or play catch-up after a long vacation or business trip, and that's understandable. But a standard weekly work schedule of 40 to 50 hours is plenty.

If you are at work 60 to 70 hours a week every week, and if you jump up from the dinner table to answer your cell phone every time it rings, put the kids to bed and then plant yourself behind your computer at home to do more work until 10 or 11 o'clock at night, it is time to ask yourself: "What kind of life is this?" What about your family? What about your friends? What about your time to rest your brain for another busy day tomorrow? Again, I've seen marriages, families and lives destroyed in some salespeople's climb to the top. When they get there, they realize they have hit rock bottom.

- Stay in good health. Aside from air traffic controllers, I can think of few jobs as stressful as a career in commissioned sales. Countless studies have shown how job stress takes its toll on your health. If your health is poor, or if you are always tired or tense, you simply cannot perform at your "Green Zone" peak.

  Get enough rest each night. Eat a healthy breakfast. Avoid a lot of fast foods at lunch. Take a few mini-breaks throughout the day to stretch, enjoy a quick walk outside, or just close your eyes and meditate for a few moments. Schedule time for your daily run, for hitting the gym, or for your yoga class...and stick to it! Your body is a living, working machine. Don't work it to death.

- Take time off. Tom, as salesman I once worked with, confessed that he and his wife hadn't taken a vacation in more than three years. I asked him why. His answer was priceless: "When business is good, I can't afford to be gone. And when business is bad, I can't afford to go!"

There will *never* be a perfect time to take a vacation; you just have to plan it and do it. Whether it's a couple of weeks here and there or several small three-day vacations spaced throughout the year, time *away* from your work serves a vital purpose.

Success in selling is hard (remember that lesson?) You need time off to relax and recharge. And when you take those vacations—unplug! Carrying your laptop, cell phone and everything else with you so you can be in constant contact and check messages isn't much of a vacation at all. Hey, do you do that now? Come on! Get a life already!

• Protect your relationships. There are people in your personal life that make you who you are and give you purpose for being on this planet. Don't ignore them for the sake of making a few more bucks. Your husband, wife, boyfriend, girlfriend, significant other, brother, sister, mom, dad, grandkids and friends all enjoy the pleasure of your company. Stay in touch, stay close, and stay connected. Don't permit your job and career to sever the ties that bind you to this life.

# Green Zone Selling

Let's do another little review:

» **You are really in business for yourself—and you should run it like you own it. To run any successful business you need to have and follow a business plan.**

» **Act like an entrepreneur. An entrepreneur is someone who shifts time and resources out of activities and areas of lower yield into activities and areas of higher yield.**

» **Although success comes at a price, don't make the price you pay for success your life, your health and your soul. Strike a balance between work…and everything else.**

The future is now. Today is the tomorrow you thought about yesterday. Make the changes you need to make now and the results you want will happen much sooner.

# Building Wealth

So far we've talked a lot about making money in your sales career. Now let's talk about keeping it. There's a big difference between earning money and building wealth. I've met many sales professionals who take home a six-figure income and still live paycheck to paycheck. If that's not what you want, you'll need to be as skilled at managing your money as you are at making it.

Financial health is important to everyone, but especially important to commissioned salespeople. Why? Because commissioned salespeople can't rely on a steady paycheck and a predictable income. It fluctuates. You might earn $80,000 one year, $150,000 the next and $65,000 the year after that. "Living within your means" becomes not a nicety, but a necessity. Just like you need a plan to manage your business, you need a plan to manage your finances.

I'm not in a position to offer expert financial advice. If you want professional guidance, talk with a qualified financial planner who has built the proper credentials to offer that counsel. However, having worked for many years in the banking, mortgage and financial services world, I am in a good position to offer my experienced *opinions*. So here goes:

- Your monthly housing expense should not exceed 25 percent of your gross monthly income. If you are renting, this includes your apartment rent plus renter's insurance. If you are a homeowner (or planning on buying a home) this includes your principle and interest mortgage payment along with your property taxes and homeowner's insurance.

  If you think 25 percent is not enough, you're wrong. It's enough. With this formula, a quarter of every dollar you earn every day goes strictly to keeping a roof over your head. When you exceed this rule by over-renting or over-buying, and your income moves backwards even slightly, you can find yourself in serious financial trouble.

- Your total monthly debt obligations (exclusive of housing) should not exceed 15 percent of your gross monthly income. This includes car payments, boat payments, student loan payments, credit cards and all other regular reoccurring monthly debt.

- You need to set aside 15 percent of your income for savings. Included here might be installments to your 401k Plan at work, your IRA, annuity plan, investments and retirement programs. This also includes regular savings account deposits and putting some money away for down times in your sales career. Having a "cushion" here gives you piece of mind. As I mentioned just a moment ago, a commissioned salesperson's income fluctuates year-by-year and it's not predictable. When business is booming and your income is up, it's always a smart idea to set aside funds for potentially slower times.

- You should park 5 percent of your income in your vacation fund. As you know, selling is a stressful and demanding job. If you are a top performer in your profession, you are working longer and harder than most. You need time off. You need to relax and recharge. If you are married or have a family, you need to stay close to them. And you need money for regular vacations to do just that.

- You should plan to invest 5 percent of your gross monthly income back into your business. Perhaps you work for a company that takes care of your marketing, client entertainment and customer contact expenses. Perhaps you don't. You'll need money for things like client gifts, holiday cards, sponsorships, personal advertising and fees to attend various conferences, conventions and learning events. You may also want to buy or upgrade your technology tools that help you run your successful sales business. If you have the funds set aside you are more inclined to spend them.

• You should consider allocating 5 percent of your annual income for philanthropy. These donations might include your favorite charitable causes, school fund drives, civic organizations and giving to your place of worship. (Some faiths request or even require a higher tithe. Use your heart as your guide here.) You are blessed to have what you have and earn what you earn. It feels good to give money to important causes you believe in and help others who are not so fortunate.

• That leaves you with 30 percent of your income for all the other stuff you want or need. These are best known as "living expenses" and include items like groceries, gas for your car, going out to dinner, playing golf, buying new clothes, taking the kids to a ball game, and a thousand other things you regularly spend your hard-earned money on.

This income budgeting plan is a guide to follow and is best illustrated with an example. Ed is a salesperson, single, and earning $60,000 a year or $5,000 a month. Using this formula his budget would be:

| | |
|---|---|
| Housing | $1,250 |
| Debt | $750 |
| Savings | $750 |
| Vacations | $250 |
| Business | $250 |
| Charity | $250 |
| Living expenses | $1,500 |
| **TOTAL** | **$5,000** |

Perhaps this describes how you are allocating your income now. Good for you! Keep it up! Perhaps, however, you are light years from this model. If so, your first inclination is to say: "This is unrealistic. Nobody can do this!" You are wrong. People *are* doing this. I do this. That means you can too.

Although most of the budget items are suggestions or guidelines, the first two are firm maximums. When you start spending over 40 percent of your income on basic housing and monthly debt obligations, you are in dangerous financial territory. The recent events with the nation's credit crisis and the meltdown of the financial and housing market were both triggered by consumers spending more on their monthly housing and debt expenses than they could afford. When you live far above your means you've got your head in the clouds and you can't see reality. You are earning money but not building any wealth. You have little or nothing left over for vacations, investing in your business, savings, charity and those day-to-day expenses of everyday life. Before long you are in a heap of trouble. Your bills pile up, you struggle to make utility and car payments, you may even wind up in bankruptcy or foreclosure. Don't think it can't happen to you. That's what the thousands of people now in bankruptcy and foreclosure once thought. (And a lot of them are salespeople!)

Here's the deal: If you can learn how to earn money, you can teach yourself how to manage that money and build a safe, secure and enjoyable life.

# Curves on the Road Ahead

Remember back when you were 15 or 16 and got your driver's license? It's only natural that when you started out driving you looked down at the road just beyond the hood of your car. You quickly learned that it's much better (and safer) to look further out in front toward the horizon. That way you can see more of your surroundings and be ready to react to what's coming toward you.

Too many salespeople go through their jobs and careers looking down at the work in front of them. They get buried in today's tasks and never see tomorrow's opportunities or problems coming. As a result, they miss the "curve" ahead.

No industry or sales job is a straight line. The road is full of dips, detours, curves, on and off-ramps. Smart salespeople see these changes and opportunities coming. Do you? Here's an interesting little test:

1. *What is one major change you see coming to your job, company or industry in the very near future?*
2. *What are you planning to do about it?*

Perhaps a major player has entered your market as a formidable competitor. What is your response? It could be that your company is about to introduce a highly-anticipated new product with big potential. Do you have your sales strategy in place for the day it launches? Maybe your office or district is downsizing your sales support staff soon. What's your plan? Highly-successful salespeople are rarely blindsided by change. They not only see change coming, but they are proactive in dealing with these curves in their careers.

Case studies are an interesting way of testing your strategic thinking as a salesperson. Let's try one now. Ready? Here goes:

You are a salesperson working at company A. The word on the street is that your firm is about to be acquired by company B, a long-standing and noble competitor. Internal scuttlebutt says senior management wants to merge the two entities and try to retain the better salespeople from both companies. That's the good news. The bad news is that if that happens, you must share your market and territory with at least one or two other salespeople from company B. Your prospects, leads and opportunities have the potential to be cut by two-thirds. And if your business drops because of this and you don't meet quota, being a salesperson from the "acquired" company, you'll likely be the first to be let go.

What would you do? (Seriously, this is a good exercise. Put the book down for a few minutes and think about how you would approach this situation.)

What did you decide? If your answer was: "I'll just wait and see what happens," you are half way out the door. Salespeople who "wait and see what happens" are often victims of circumstances like this all the time. The curve came, they missed it, and they crashed.

Really good salespeople look down the road ahead and are ready to act. That's another application of operating in the Green Zone of your future in selling. So, I'll ask you again:

1. *What is one change you see coming to your job, company or industry in the very near future?*
2. *What are you planning to do about it?*

# Managing Your Career in Sales

Imagine living in Los Angeles and taking a business trip to New York City. First, you get in your car and drive to the airport. You park your car and take a shuttle bus to the terminal. From there you board a plane to Chicago, switch planes, and board another flight to New York. Upon landing, you take the people-mover to the main terminal, collect your bags and hop on the subway to downtown. After exiting the train station, you hail a cab to your hotel. One trip, seven different vehicles to get you where you want to go.

Think of your sales career as a "business trip" and the jobs you work in as "vehicles." It is extremely rare for a top salesperson to achieve a long and successful sales career in a single job or with a single employer. The jobs you hold are merely vehicles you use to get you where you want to go.

It can be a fatal career error to become stuck in a certain job or with a specific employer for too long. This is often the beginning of a dead end. Your goal should not be to have a successful job in sales but a successful *career in selling*. In today's marketplace and world economy, it is highly likely you will outlive your current employer. (Thinking back, I worked for seven different organizations in my career before launching my own company. Six of the seven are no longer in business…and I still am!)

One very successful salesperson I know started out selling hair care products. Then she landed a job selling real estate and after a few years moved into marketing commercial warehouse space. After that she stepped into selling restaurant equipment. Now she works as a mortgage loan officer…selling money! You might think she moved around so much because she failed in these various sales jobs. On the contrary; she was *extremely* successful in every enterprise. But company closures, industry contractions, a relocating spouse and new opportunities that presented themselves facilitated her many moves. Patti has earned a great deal of money over the years and transferred her selling skills into each new role. Today, after almost twenty years in selling, she is a well-rounded and artful salesperson that any organization would be lucky to have on their team. Patti understands what managing a successful career in selling is all about.

See yourself not as a hair care sales rep or a real estate agent or a restaurant equipment salesperson or a loan officer or anything else but a *career sales professional*. Do that and you can excel in selling at just about any company in any industry for the rest of your life.

# Green Zone Selling

To quickly recap the primary points you just learned:

» **There is a difference between earning money and building wealth. If you are smart enough to make good money, be smart enough to know how to manage it.**

» **There are always curves in the road of any sales career. Look down the horizon and watch for obstacles and opportunities. Never be blindsided by changes you knew were coming. Have a plan to respond.**

» **This is *your* career in selling and it is up to you to manage it. Great selling skills are transferable to a number of other businesses. Keep your options open and don't allow yourself to get too entrenched in one job, one company or one industry.**

There are three more lessons to learn in The Future Zone. Here they are...

# Find Your Motivation

I will begin the last three lessons of this book with a question that requires serious thought. This is a "riddle" you must solve and solve completely if you are to enjoy a long, fulfilling career in sales. You say you want to be a success in selling? Then answer this:

*Why do you want to be successful?*

Focus on that question for a moment. Why do you want to be successful? What's your motivation for success? We've all heard and used the word "motivation" a million times in our lives. But do you know what it means?

Here is how I break down the word motivation: "Motive" means *reason* and "-ation" is a suffix implying *action*. So, the definition of motivation is the *reason* for the *action*. For a woman to go on a diet she needs the motivation or a good reason why. For a man to improve his golf game, he needs to be motivated, or have a good reason why. Without a compelling *reason*, neither will ever take the *action* and achieve what they want.

I have the privilege of speaking at dozens of conferences and conventions every year. Sometimes the host or emcee will introduce me as a "motivational speaker." I hate that. I am not a motivational speaker—never have been, never will be. Just the thought runs counter to what I have always believed:

*You can't motivate people.*
*People can only motivate themselves.*

If you are an unmotivated person and have been for some time, listening to me speak for 90 minutes won't change your attitude or your life. If you are already a motivated person, listening to me speak for 90 minutes won't make any difference either; you're already motivated! I see myself not as a motivational speaker but an "activational" speaker. (My own word; I made it up!) I can't give people their *reason* to want to succeed. But if people have a reason to want to succeed, I can point them in the right direction of the *action* they need to take. If I can help them to do that, I've done my job as a speaker. As I tell my audiences:

> *"My job is to help you
> do something new tomorrow
> that you weren't doing yesterday
> as a result of being here with me today."*

That's not motivation, it's activation! Those people who leave my session and take action are *motivated*. Those who don't are not. Let's not complicate things any more than that.

The point I want to hammer home is that motivation comes from inside you and nowhere else. Don't expect other things and other people to motivate you. Seminars don't motivate. Books don't motivate. CDs don't motivate. Your colleagues will not motivate you. Even your boss can't motivate you to do things. (Bosses can threaten you or inspire you or help you—but they can't *make* you do something if you won't do it.)

Motivation—like faith, integrity, hope, trust and attitude—are all internal. *We* define them, *we* control them. To be a success in selling, you have to be able to motivate yourself to do what needs to be done. And to create that motivation, you need to have persuasive, personal reasons why you need to be successful.

- You say you want to make more money. *Why?*
- You say you want to raise your sales results. *Why?*
- You say you want to be a top producer in your company. *Why?*

If you can't come up with a solid answer to each of these

questions you will never achieve any of these goals because in your heart and head you haven't articulated *why* they are important to you. Your motivation will drive your success all throughout your career and it will determine how far and high you will eventually go.

We have discovered here in *Green Zone Selling* that positive action leads to positive results. But what's going to get *you* to take the action to get the results you desire? What's your motivation? Again:

*Why do you want to be successful?*

Take out a sheet of paper and write on the top: "I want to be a success!" Below that, write down at least three good reasons why. Do that right now. (This is a powerful exercise I have conducted many times in my sales seminars. It is amazing how many people can't come up with three reasons why they want to be successful!) Go beyond simple, obvious answers like: "Make more money." Really put some grey matter to work here and develop at least three gripping reasons why you want to be a success at what you do.

Since I always practice the ideas I preach, I did this exercise myself. I too want to be a success. Here are my three reasons why:

1. I have a family to support. I want my wife to live in a beautiful home, drive a nice car, eat at great restaurants and wear high-quality clothes. I want my son and daughter to enjoy wonderful vacations, go to good colleges and never want for basic necessities. I want to make sure we have more-than-adequate health care coverage and a savings cushion to fall back on. I am the breadwinner of the family, and I learned long ago you need a lot of bread to support a family well.

2.  I don't want to work forever. My goal is to semi-retire at age 60 and fully retire at 62…not that far from now. Retiring at a younger age means getting to play golf, hike in our national parks and travel the world to see new lands and cultures while I am still relatively young and healthy. I want to be able to enjoy the "golden years" of my life to the fullest—instead of getting up every morning and dragging myself into work until I drop dead.

3.  I have an ego to feed. I enjoy being recognized for my accomplishments. I get goose bumps when people call or email me to let me know what I taught them helped transform their sales careers. Being successful in my profession means being liked and admired by my colleagues and clients, and although that has never put a penny in my pocket, it feels really, really good!

Those are three strong reasons why I want to be successful. They get me out of bed each morning and drive me forward in my work every day. What are your reasons? *Why do you want to be successful?* The answers, my friend, are *your* motivation.

# The High Five

Relationships are central to your success. If you agree with that statement—and I cannot image you wouldn't—ask yourself this:

> *What am I doing, right now,*
> *to maintain and grow the relationships*
> *that are most important to me?*

We know that selling is a people business. But "people" does not just refer to your prospects and customers. I want to talk about the *other* people you spend your time with—the people who are also central to your success.

"No man is an island," John Donne once wrote in his famous poem. By the same measure, no salesperson can go it alone. You need people to help you, to support you and to encourage you. You need people to inspire you, celebrate success with you and hold you accountable for your actions. These people include your friends, family, suppliers, vendors, co-workers, managers—anybody who is in a position to influence your success in one way or another. These people are every bit as important to your success as your prospects and customers; they are your *team*.

One more exercise (this will be the last one!) I call this exercise the "High Five." Here we go:

*Make a list of the five people in your life
who have the greatest influence on your success.*

Do that now. Who influences your success—good or bad, positive or negative—the most? Who impacts how you think, how you feel, how you work and how you operate your business every day? You only get five names on your list, so choose wisely.

When you've got that done, stare at your list of names. Then start asking yourself some very pointed and private questions:

- Who on this list is a positive influence on me?
- Who is a negative influence on me?
- Who do I have a great relationship with?
- Who do I have a so-so relationship with?
- Who do I have a poor relationship with?
- Who on this list should not be there?
- Who needs to be on this list but is not?
- Do the people who support me know how much I appreciate them?

In sales, we talk a lot about "relationship management." Certainly, it is a terrific idea to build, grow and sustain great relationships with your customers and clients. The same holds true with your own personal success team. Look at your High Five list again. *What are you doing, right now, to build, grow and sustain great relationships with the five people who have the greatest influence on your success?*

# Bridging the Gap

As we come to the end of our journey together, I want to share with you a final bit of personal perspective. It's something I picked up long ago and carried with me throughout my career. It is this:

*Knowledge is knowing what to do.*
*Skill is knowing how to do it.*
*Success comes from knowing that you've done it.*

There are two gaps you must bridge to become an even greater success in selling. The first gap is the gap between *not knowing* and *knowing*. Some salespeople are not as successful as they could be because they just don't know *how* to be successful. I call this a "can't do" problem. The reason for this gap is the salesperson's lack of knowledge and/or skill level. Many salespeople have never been taught how to pick up the phone and land an appointment. Many have never learned how to conduct an effective client conversation, manage their time, build a sales plan, or deliver a solid presentation. Many have yet to discover the right way to provide superior, memorable service to keep customers coming back. These are not bad people; they are often good people with great intentions who don't have the knowledge or skills to properly perform the job. If they just knew what to do and how to do it, they would be doing it. They can't because they don't know how!

One of my aims with this book is to bridge that gap between not knowing and knowing. I've presented more than fifty skills, approaches, techniques and behaviors you can put into practice right away. (Even without the benefit of this book, with all the other great seminars, books, CDs, DVDs, magazines, newsletters and help available out there today on the art and science of selling, there's no plausible excuse for a salesperson going through his or her career not knowing what they are doing.)

The second gap you must bridge to achieve greater success is the gap between *knowing* and *doing*. There are thousands of salespeople out there today that know exactly what to do. They just aren't doing it! Maybe it's apathy. Maybe it's laziness. Maybe they are simply complacent—not happy with where they are but not motivated enough to do something about it.

If having the desire or motivation is the issue, the solution lies within. This is the other side of the coin; not a "can't do" problem but a "won't do" problem. It is one thing to own the skills and knowledge you need to be a success in selling; it is a far different thing to be doing what you need to do. I cannot force you to use the concepts, skills and ideas you have learned here or anywhere else. I can only strongly suggest that you do. As Andrew Carnegie—who was the success story featured in Napoleon Hill's book *Think and Grow Rich*—said: *"You cannot push a man up a ladder. He must be willing to climb himself."*

I truly hope the lessons in this book have inspired you to take action. Above all, remember this:

*Knowledge is power, but only action transforms.*

A very wise man once said: "When all is said and done, more is always said than done." Talk is cheap. As a matter of fact, it's free. It's one thing to talk about how much you know and what you plan to do or what you should be doing. *It is a far, far better thing to be doing it.*

I am excited for you; I mean that. When I see a positive attitude married to potential in someone, and when I can help that someone make the decision to change his or her life for the better, I am personally rewarded. Believe me when I say you can improve your standing. You can increase your income. You can empower yourself to become an even greater success in selling. You can spend the rest of your career in the Green Zone and enjoy everything it offers. The only thing that could possibly stand in your way now is your ability to act—to put into practice everything that you have learned.

There are millions of highly-successful sales professionals around the world. I have met thousands of them over the past 30 years. Let me tell you something: *they are no more special than you.* They are ordinary people who achieved extraordinary results by transforming knowledge into action. They live rich and rewarding lives. They contribute positively and productively to their families, to society, to their customers and to the companies where they work. They are happy, fulfilled, and personally proud of what they have accomplished.

You have the power to join their ranks. There is no reason to wait. Time marches on and we are all blessed with a precious but brief moment on this Earth. Make it happen today. This is your life. Your time is *now.*

# Green Zone Selling

Here are the final three lessons that should never be forgotten:

» **Motivation is the reason behind the action. What are your reasons for wanting to become a greater success? Answer that question and you will find your motivation.**

» **The "High Five" are the five people who have the greatest influence on your success. Know who they are and work hard to build, grow and sustain great relationships with these people on your team.**

» **Knowledge is power, but only action transforms. You have learned dozens of great approaches, ideas, techniques and selling skills in this book. But knowing them will not make a difference. It is up to you to put them into practice.**

Your career in selling is what you make it. Congratulations on your plans to become an even greater success. Welcome to the Green Zone!

**Do you know someone who would enjoy this book?
Order a copy for them today!**

You may complete the form below and mail or fax it to us
or you can visit **www.GreenZoneSelling.com** and order online.

---

### Order Form

# of copies _____ @ $23 each

Includes shipping and handling

(For discounts on book orders of 10 or more
please contact us at 877.430.2329.)

Name: _____

Company: _____

Street:_____

City:_____

State/Zip: _____

Phone: _____

Email: _____

If paying by check, please remit and mail payment to:
**Douglas Smith & Associates**
408 Coopers Hawk Drive
Biltmore Park
Asheville, NC 28803

If paying by credit card
(MasterCard, Visa, American Express):

Name as it appears on card: _____

Card number:_____

Expiration date: _____

Zip code for credit card bill: _____

You may mail credit card orders to the above address or
fax your order to our secure fax line at 866.534.4567

**Looking for a great speaker to address the
sales professionals in your organization?**

Doug Smith is showing companies and sales
professionals how to find more customers, make more
money and become more successful...right now!

Doug's high-impact workshops, webinars, sales
training programs and keynote presentations
deliver valuable content with practical application.
His seminar and presentation topics include:

*Rising to the Top*
*Selling Your Competitive Edge*
*Turning Time into Money*
*Mastering Your Selling Skills*
*Coaching Sales Performance*
*And more than 20 others*

For more information on Doug Smith's resources,
visit **www.DougSmithPresents.com**
or call Douglas Smith & Associates at
**877.430.2329**
or email Doug Smith directly at
**Doug@GreenZoneSelling.com**